It is Not A Spiritual Thing

- Verbal Abuse -

LADY DAY

ISBN: 1-4392-3291-1
EAN13: 9781439232910

For clarification, any writing in this book that is enclosed in brackets indicate not only a break in thought, but also my present thought or reflection on what was previously stated. The Lord wants us to consider that "…with all thy getting, get an understanding" (Proverbs 4:7)

"TO MY READERS…In my rush to tell my story, I know I have made some mistakes in my manuscript. Please overlook the typos and understand the words written are sincerely from my heart. If you can embrace the message I have endeavored to impart, I know you will be blessed!" Lady Day

Table of Contents

Acknowledgments

I wish to acknowledge every church, every pastor, (especially my current pastor and his wife), every saint (a believer in the body of Christ) every man, woman and child I have known who has touched my life. I am the better because of who you are and because of what you have meant to me.

My mother, my children, my sisters and brother; my grandchildren, my cousins, aunts and uncles; nieces and nephews have each played a pivotal role no one else could have played. I love each of you and THANK God for YOUR place in MY LIFE.

I have become a great woman because I have overcome some great odds in order to find my way in this world. I thank God for the challenges and for the victories I have experienced.

To the lives I have touched and the ones I will touch here after, I wish to thank you now and in advance and I trust God will bless you and keep you in His loving care!

— *Lady Day*

I Wish to Dedicate This Book in Loving Memory of....

My eldest brother, Richard Jr. (2005)

My father, Richard Sr. (1998)

My two grandchildren, Shane & Sierra (1998)

My Uncle Henry (1997)

and

My Sunshine (1991)

Introduction

In the home I grew up in, my father was so domineering, his wife, children, grandchildren and great-grandchildren all feared him. I do not believe he has ever missed a day of putting my mother down in 50 years of marriage. Her response to him was always the same— acceptance. I, too, was an object of his verbal abuse since early childhood. My sister (12 years older than I), was married by the time my father's verbal assaults had escalated. My other sister (2 years younger than I), has no recollection of dad calling her out of her name. I don't know about my brothers (one 9 years younger and the other 10 years younger than I), whether they were cursed out when they were younger. But both of them had a different opinion of our dad when they became adults. However, it was the behavior of my mother that made me wonder.

My mother would hum a spiritual song while my dad would follow her around the house, calling her anything but a child of God. I knew that he was wrong but my mother demanded respect for her husband, no matter what he said or did. It was just "his way." I was supposed to love him simply because he was my father. I was not to question his behavior or something had to be wrong with me. Mom often reminded me of what God said in His Word (the Bible)—"We are to LOVE our enemies"—and that's exactly what she was trying to do—to the extent that loving and respecting her self was totally left out of the equation.

I was too young to understand that I would hail my mother as the epitome of sainthood and my dad as the devil incarnate. I did not realize that my decision to condone this disrespect from my father would lead to giving my husband permission to verbally assault me as well. For one partner to systematically persecute another partner is wrong. Behavior that controls another person through fear and humiliation is ABUSE, whether it is verbal or physical.

Each Christian has a ministry. My message is to those who have a personal relationship with JESUS, and think it is spiritual to live in an environment that debases and frightens them. It is not a spiritual thing for someone to call you out of your name; to subject yourself to mental anguish—and wait for God to help you. THAT IS LIVING IN HELL! The wicked shall be turned into Hell... (Psalms 9:17)—NOT THE SAINTS! It is foolish and unscriptural to believe you are suffering for righteousness sake, when you are being mentally or emotionally wounded.

Today, there are women (and some men) who are praying daily to be set free from verbally abusive relationships. They do not know they already have the power TO STOP IT. But this book will not only encourage my sisters (and brothers in the Lord); this book will encourage ANYONE who recognizes their tendency to embrace a verbally abusive lifestyle. The answer is the same. You too have the power TO STOP IT.

Verbal abuse may be an international phenomenon; a national problem or a demented cultural lifestyle; but it is not, nor will I ever call it A SPIRITUAL THING!

•   •   •

Part One

TRUSTING OTHERS

Now I Pronounce You Man & Wife

(How Could This Happen To Me??)

CHAPTER 1

If a man (significant other) calls you out of your name, check him. If he apologizes and doesn't do it again, then he respects you and will continue to respect you. If a man calls you out of your name, and you check him—and he apologizes (or doesn't apologize), but calls you out of your name again, he has no respect for you. Get out of his life and never go back!!!!!

– My late great, Uncle Henry

I married my children's father, June 21, 1969. It did not take me a long time to discover my husband had a similar habit of hurling verbal assaults at me, just like my dad. When the physical abuse (or accidents) started, I really could not figure out what was going on. It began when he shoved me, then he apologized. At some point, I heard the declaration of a threat. Of course, an apology followed it too. Then there was a slap and another apology.

Then one day he slapped my face extremely hard. It should have been accompanied by an apology, a hug, or a kiss to relieve the pain. *But, there was no apology and no hug. There was nothing to soothe the shock I felt.* However, some sharp words came through his lips on that day—that I will always remember; **"THAT WAS NO ACCIDENT!"** There was no doubt in my mind; I knew I was in trouble. He said he did not owe me an apology because he was NOT sorry. I had deserved it.

At that moment, I became the third generation of abused women in my family. My maternal grandmother had been verbally and physically abused by my grandfather; my mother was verbally abused by my father; and I was verbally abused and physically battered by my husband. I did not realize that when I gave him permission to call me out of my name—I was in fact, giving him permission to abuse me physically as well. Those vicious words he had uttered–were the precursor–a definite warning of things to come.   (You see, I believe verbal abuse precedes physical abuse.)

I did not know I would be walking on egg shells during most of my marriage. *I never knew I would be slapped often; beaten with his fist; pushed; shoved; my eyes blackened; dragged through the house; or dragged and kicked out of the bed more often than I care to remember.   I did not know he would threaten me with knives around my throat.   I had no way of knowing he would place guns to my head and threaten to kill me many times.   How could I know that once he removed the weapon, he would force me to have sex with him because he preferred* sex with me under duress?   No one told me I was in a conjugal warfare.

No one explained to me that the extra-marital affairs would be endless.   There was always some proof left around my home, my bed, or the car that someone else was sharing him with me.   It became a regular occurrence to find nasty undergarments in one of those three places.   I even found a vibrator with human hair wrapped around it.   Never knowing when or where I would find such objects, filled me with dread, dismay, and/or trepidation.   Because I had been advised to ignore these occurrences, I would just wrap them up in newspaper and throw them away.   Then I would pretend they never happened.

Then, there were the calls, where the person on the other end would say nothing whenever I answered the telephone, and then hang up.   Still other times, though few in number, I would actually hear my husband talking to the other woman, and I would quietly hang up the receiver. I have been so scared, I was too afraid to run and too afraid to stand still. I was too frightened to tell and too frightened not to tell. Some of things that were done to me; and some of the things he said to me were too repugnant to remember; so I simply made myself forget.

THE REASON FOR THE SEASON

At the beginning of this chapter I paraphrased a saying my favorite uncle use to say. With all the studies and conferences that study domestic violence, throughout the world and in our own backyard, none could say it better than he. Verbal abuse comes from a TOTAL DISRESPECT for the other person. I believe a **VERBAL ABUSER is an individual who uses name calling to control another person, bringing them under subjection or obedience to him (or her).**

I ALSO BELIEVE TO ENDURE IT is to somehow justify it–to admit whatever is being said to you is somehow accurate. Small wonder an abuser feels it is OK, in most cases, to say anything they wish to the recipient of their harsh words. Cursing people out has unofficially become a **normal way of life** in our homes, in our schools, on the radio, television and in the movies. It is what we do with little (or total) regard for our children. Then when our children emulate us, we wonder "What's their problem?"

Some people like my mother said she has never been hurt or upset by what my dad called her. But I say she is lying and do not even know it. In fact, I am willing to believe that a whole lot of people will say the same thing and has at some point chosen to remain in that kind of lifestyle.

I can now say I was living in TOTAL IGNORANCE AND ACTED LIKE A TOTAL FOOL.   To permit someone to have that kind of control over me meant I DID NOT LOVE OR RESPECT MYSELF. I cannot demand from others what I fail to give myself.

I DIDN'T SEE IT COMING

During our brief courtship, I seemed unable to express myself.   Although I was better educated than he, my high school diploma never prepared me for this. I never felt like a whole person around him. The putdowns he jokingly continued to render, ONLY REMINDED ME OF HOW IMPERFECT I WAS. In the presence of others, I was always the butt of the joke. Now this occurred before I married him and still, I **did not get it!**

Had I checked him like my uncle said some nineteen years later, I would have never allowed myself to be caught up with the drama I endured. For instance, I later learned that saying nothing to my children's father—was not good advice. If evidence of infidelity was found in *MY HOUSE, I SHOULD HAVE SAID SOMETHING TO MY SPOUSE. TO IGNORE IT, WAS TO ACCEPT IT AS A PART OF MY LIFE.* When your self-esteem is troubled, your mind is also affected.

Had I known that practically everyone I was around at that time, in our circle of family and friends, was going through the same thing or a similar scenario, I would never have taken their advice. Now, I understand that if you can not stop the violence in your home, how could you help me? The blind cannot lead the blind or they will both fall into a ditch (Matt. 15:16).

VERBAL ABUSE IS A LIFESTYLE

So, I endured a lifestyle I abhorred, living in stark fear for fifteen years of my young adult life. [What I did not realize is that verbal abuse is a lifestyle.] When I was married to my children's father, I did not walk the streets nor did I sleep with other men. I did not use curse words, smoke, drink, or use mind altering drugs. I was a good woman. *My only fault was that I loved God and did not know I was not a "bitch" or a "whore": I did not even know I deserved better. I never deserved the abuse I so quietly accepted. Moreover, from all the evidence, I was living in a hellish situation. God created Hell for the devil and his angels. If my husband was the devil, why was I trying, with all my might and strength to live in hell with him?*

I was prime meat for this kind of relationship— I was the prey and my ex-*husband was the beast. He may have been the sick one, <u>but my toleration of such disrespect made me just as ill.</u>*

The question can now be asked, ***"How can a God-fearing woman allow herself to be caught up in such an unspeakable situation.*** *How could such a disaster last for 15 years?"* I believe it took a combination of things to get in such a mess:

1. My immediate family took first place because they helped define how I was raised. It was in my parental home where I learned to feel good or bad about myself.

2. My environment took second place because it was who I was around, outside of my immediate family.   Whether it was my extended family or my neighborhood, it is where I had to learn to exist, outside of my home. Moreover, it helped to re-enforce who I was to become.

3. The church took third place because everyone is not raised in a family that teaches bible principles on a regular basis. Because I was taught by a Christian mother, the church played a tremendous part in my belief system. It is also where I learned to spiritualize a lot of things in my life.

4.   I was afraid to think for myself. Ultimately, my admiration for self did not surpass my admiration for others.

5.   By not recognizing when I WAS BEING VERBALLY INJURED, made it difficult for me to choose who I should allow into my life.

6. I did not recognize the damage verbal abuse caused me and others.

7. I did not know how to take the personal responsibility needed to change my life and my attitude.

8. I did not understand I had to validate myself. I earnestly sought others to validate me because I felt I just was not good enough to do it for myself.

9. I did not love myself. *I learned to hate* **everything** about me.

When a significant other is in your life, you are bringing two worlds together and it is to be taken seriously as if your life depended on it. The last report I heard over the radio in November, 2008 said this economy is going to increase the number of domestic abuse cases here in the United States. WE REALLY NEED TO RECOGNIZE!

Moreover, throughout my courtship, I was never cognizant of him exhibiting the same attitude my father exhibited towards me—I mean I recognized the similarities—but I never paid enough attention to it to challenge it. My goodness, I did not know there was a problem; nor did I know that it COULD be addressed. What I did not understand is that my thinking WAS A NATURAL RESULT OF MY UPBRINGING. It was...

. . .

All In The Family

(It REALLY IS A Family Affair)

CHAPTER 2

When my great-nephew stood up to my dad and stumped his little foot, he told my dad he was a "mean man." He put his little hands on his little waist and stumped his little foot again and looked up at his granddad and said "You are a mean man!" He did this several times. My dad looked at this little person in amazement and walked inside his bedroom. My mother took her great-grandson by the hand and tried to tell him how wrong he was. I interceded for him. "Mother, you should pat him on the head and say keep 'up the good work'. The child is right. You should give him a piece of cake and let him know that he was right." I told him, "You did a good job because granddad is a mean man." My mother looked at me in bewilderment as I sent him out to play. I simply wish someone in my family had interceded for me.

– My Personal Reflection

No wonder I could not remember when the verbal abuse began in the marriage. The putdowns began in my parental home, and I learned to accept it as a NORMAL part of my life. I was about the age of six when the verbal abuse towards me began. It centered on an eye condition that I developed about that time.

HEARING BUT SEEING NO ONE

One day during a school recess, somehow I had a terrible fall. I don't know whether someone pushed me down or if I just fell off the playground equipment. It had to be a hard fall because when I got up, I felt a little dazed. It did not take me long to realize I could not see—everything around me was in TOTAL DARKNESS. I could still hear the voices of the other children playing, but I could not see anyone.

I started to scream as loud as I could for someone to help me—as I slowly fell back on the ground—afraid no one would hear me. I was petrified that no one would see the predicament I was in.   I was screaming for my mom until a man came and picked me up; then I started crying for my dad. I was simply terrified. Apparently, he took me to the school's main office where my parents were called, because before long I heard my mother's voice and felt her warmth. She and I were transported, I later learned, to Chicago's Eye and Ear Clinic.

It seemed like I was in darkness for an eternity as eye drop medication was administered to me, and I was asked several times, "Can you see?"   After awhile, the darkness lightened, then there was blurriness and finally, I could see again. Not long after that, I developed an eye condition called Strabismus or Tropia. The muscles in my left eye were too weak to pull the eye straight; so my left eye turned towards my nose, or my eye was crossed (on a constant basis).

Some people have this problem, and it cannot be corrected except through surgery (Strabotomy).   Fortunately for me, wearing glasses made my eye appear straight. However, when my glasses were off, that eye would turn in again. I was so conscious about "my crossed eye," that if my glasses came off accidentally (while playing at school, for instance), I would act as if I had gone stone blind. I would close my eyes and start crying hysterically until someone would give me my glasses back. If my glasses or lens broke (which did not happen often—because I guarded those glasses with my life), I would have to be taken home because I pretended to be blind—keeping my eyes shut because I didn't want anyone to see what I looked like without them.

I'M SORRY!

Even though I was only six, I already knew children and some adults could be really cruel. Being called out of my name became a common occurrence in my home. I would often take my glasses off at home because I wasn't use to wearing them and because I thought I did not need them on (when I wasn't around *other people)*. You see I could still see and read without my glasses.   So I felt I did not need them on constantly; until my father started to tell me how ugly I had become.

He started calling me names like "cross-eyed fool" or "yella crossed-eyed niggah". The repetitiveness of those words would soon wound me in a way, I could never have imagined. Those words would become an intricate part of who I would become.   *All I knew as a child is that I wanted so much to be loved and accepted.* But, as time passed, I would later learn my need to be loved and accepted would cost me—my precious individuality.   Not feeling the love and care of my parents, in the world I was growing up in, explains why as a child I spent so much time in front of the television (*in a world outside of my own)*.

Television was still relatively new in 1956, and it became a past time of mine. It *was the one place I could escape to, and dream of being anyone I wanted to be*—since in my world, I "never had a chance of amounting to anything." I felt I would never be quite good enough." I was always totally into any sitcom or movie I would be watching. [Today, I am the same way when it comes to watching a good movie in particular. More often than not, I am watching and hearing every single detail—meaning I can not hear anyone else speaking to me. I cannot tell you how that habit took its toll in my marriage.]

At first, while looking at the television, I would wear my glasses, but sometimes I would take them off. My father would seem to come out from nowhere; his loud voice screaming at me to put the "goddamn glasses back on my goddamn face." I learned to find my glasses quickly, put them back on and get out of his way—while trying to tell him how sorry I was (for not wearing my glasses). Sometimes, I would return to my television show, but generally, I would not. Lord help me if I did not have my glasses with me. On several occasions my favorite comedian would come on and me watching him with no glasses on made those occasions quite volatile.

My television idol, Mr. Jerry Lewis, crossed his eyes a lot and my father hated to see him do that. But he was so funny and I loved watching him. When he came on, I would sit real close to the TV screen as if I might miss something. My father would suddenly appear and treat me somewhat like an animal—swinging at me, hitting and kicking me away from the set. It was during these times that haunt me the most because I would not even have my glasses with me. His voice nearly scared me to death and I would panic as I tried to scoot or crawl away as fast as I could because I could not seem to get up fast enough. *Sometimes my mother would try to hold him back while telling me to get out of the room,* and *sometimes* she would join in with the name calling.

Some how my dad figured this comedian had taught me how to cross my eyes or at least encouraged me to cross mine. He theorized I practiced it so much my eye got stuck in the process. I felt my dad hated me for what I had done. He now had a serious problem looking at me, now that my eye was crossed. [*Later in my adult life, I questioned my father, to see whether he actually believed that I, had caused my eye to cross. He said he did. He never understood why I did that to myself when I was so pretty before. I explained to him that weak muscles were probably inherent in our family. It was no fault of my own. He really seemed surprised.*] I remember asking my mother one day why he couldn't just love me anyway. She told me that it hadn't always been that way;

once my dad was very proud of me. Since birth I looked just like him.

PRIDE AND JOY

I was lighter in complexion than anyone else in my family (so, they thought my light complexion made me special indeed, so I was told). I was also told as a baby he loved to take me around his friends so they could tease him. They would say things like "she could not possibly be your child, because she is too yellow and you are too black." But, when all the jesting was over, they would have to admit: "She sure is your daughter, man. She looks just like you." The old folks would say, "She looked just like you spitted her out." So, although his first born was a girl and before the eye problem took center stage, I some how felt that I might have been his PRIDE AND JOY.

[I recently asked my mom was I ever dad's favorite? She told me, I WAS NEVER his favorite. My youngest sister was ALWAYS his favorite. Then she explained to me how he would always put her in the front seat of his car and drive. She was always standing there beside him with her arm around his neck.] I personally believe children know when they are not appreciated or loved. I may not have been able to express it when I was younger, but as I grew, somehow I knew, I was never the one he adored. I have felt it most of my life. *[I guess I should just get over it, but I just this found this out—in 2008 and I don't know how to* just get over it.] *But I guess somebody had to be his favorite. It kind of makes sense in the whole scheme of things. I was a member of this family; I just did not feel like a well-loved member.*

When my eye crossed like it did, my father just *did not know how to handle it. He was simply devastated. He did not know how to handle* **this slow death. Well, from that point on, something down in me was dying right along with him.**   I can recall another moment in my life, when this same eye problem became an even greater burden to me.

THE STRAW THAT BROKE THE CAMEL'S BACK

It involved the second family portrait we took. *(The first one included my oldest nephew, who was living with us at the time. It was in black and white and I did not have the eye condition at that time.)* When we took the second portrait (which would be in color, without my nephew because my oldest sister had married and he now resided with her); I had the eye condition. But, I also had my new glasses and for me, that made everything all right. I was very excited about the new picture. Did I tell you, I would rather die than be seen without my glasses? They were my deliverance from ridicule and my salvation.

I felt my heart breaking in two when the photographer told my parents my glasses had to come off because they would cause a glare. I remember begging them to let me keep my glasses on. However, it was to no avail. The helplessness I felt was so overwhelming because I wanted so badly for this picture to be perfect. I started begging God to please straighten my eye. "Please God; do not let my eye mess up the picture!" I even asked God to help me smile as pretty as I could. When the photographer began taking the pictures, all I could do was hope and pray my eye would not cause a problem. *I wanted everyone to see how pretty I really was. So, I smiled to hide my discomfort, my disappointment, my terror, and my broken heart.*

When the pictures came back, I remember how pretty my mother told me I looked. Even dad mumbled something to that affect. However, when I saw the portraits, something inside of me felt sick. I believe that was the first time I actually entertained the thought that God did not hear my prayer. *There were only three portraits taken: one with all four of us (my parents, my youngest sister and myself); one with only my sister and one with only me. They were only 5 x 7, but to me they might as well have been 11 x 14.*

My sister's picture was simply beautiful—her coal-black hair always held its curl and the dimple in each of her cheeks made her reddish-brown complexion look so rich—like a living doll. My portrait, on the other hand, reflected my sandy-brown hair that could not hold a curl if my life depended on it. I felt my yellowish-light brown skin was overwhelmingly distinct from the rest of my family. *And my smile; my smile looked hideous to me—stretching from ear to ear, only to emphasize that left eye looking directly at my nose, while the other eye looked straight ahead.*

On the family portrait, my sister was standing on the floor between our parents and looked as if she belonged to my mother and father. In this portrait (I longed so much to look like I was a part of my family), but I simply looked like a disenfranchised orphan who knelt behind my sister's parents; one hand on my dad's shoulder and one hand on my mom's shoulder, head tilted, smiling from ear to ear, while that one eye was oblivious to the grief it left in my heart. I was so embarrassed. I had single-handedly destroyed two pictures because of the fact— I was in them.

WAITING TO EXHALE

I remember my mother framed all three pictures and put them on display somewhere near the front entrance of the house, *where everyone who entered could see them.* [Now, when I think about it, what else could she have done? *If she did not put the pictures on display, it meant they were ashamed of me.* She must have felt she had no other choice. How sad it must have been for my parents; how sad for me.]

Those pictures not only reminded me of my problem, but it permitted anyone who entered our home *to see how I really looked without my precious glasses.* This in turn left me vulnerable to a variety of ridicule. For instance, my parents were always questioned *by relatives and friends* (usually in my presence): "Why did you allow her to do this to herself?" "My God, what happened to her?" "That is a shame!" "So this is what she looks like without her glasses!" My susceptibility to comments like these laced with sarcasm, seemed endless.

I tried several times to destroy the picture of myself—but my attempts failed—my mother would catch me every time. At some point, my portrait disappeared. However, the family portrait remained. That is, until the day that I had tried my best to unsuccessfully cut my picture out with a safety pin. And then one day, it was no longer there.

The helplessness and hopelessness I felt as a young child of six or seven years of age was deeply entrenched—because my family suffered silently—because I was an embarrassment to them. This was a big part of the emotional scarring I received as a child, wherein no one was to blame. I was trying to make myself disappear so as not to cause any more grief to my family or myself. *Therefore, the eye condition was the primary reason at an early age I chose to be a* compliant child.

"Do what I am told!" "I must do it without questioning it, and maybe I will win their love". "Maybe they would not hate me so." I mean I knew my family loved me, but I could not seem to get enough of it. No matter what I did,

I could not get enough praise, enough hugs, or enough expressions of love. *Sometimes, I wondered if they were afraid to even touch me.* All I knew is I was a terrible embarrassment to them and I wanted to make things right. I was too young and too innocent to understand...

· · ·

Compliancy — Was Not The Way To Go

(Coming From A Child's Perspective)

CHAPTER 3

Through the years I have always heard my family say, "I love you, but..." I mean there was always this "BUT" attached. They did not say it, but I could hear it just the same. It is even more pronounced today than it was in years gone by. I have never understood it, but I have grown more accustomed to it. I don't know why, but I have always felt as if I have done something wrong or said the wrong thing; and yet I do not know just what I may have done or what I may have said. Perhaps it's a family thing that I alone am aware of. But it Is a contributing factor of my feelings of not being quite pretty enough or quite good enough....

– My Personal Reflection

Now, I did not just wake up one morning and became *the compliant one*. It took years of practice to think that way—to be that way. I tried so hard not to create waves in my family, but it seemed I was always doing something wrong and always making my parents angry.

WHEN I WAS A CHILD...

As a child, I did what other children did—only to find each action would earn me a name that would began defining who I was in their eyes. When I started wetting the bed, I was not only a "no good, crossed-eyed yella niggah"; I became a "nasty, no-good, crossed-eyed yella niggah."

I was merely a child who loved to play; however, I was always falling down. When I tried to skate, I fell. When I ran, I fell. When I rode my bike, I fell and bruised myself every single time. I now earned the right to be called "a nasty, no good, clumsy, crossed-eyed yella niggah" or a "clumsy fool" because I was told I could not stand up without falling down.

Moreover, I acquired the name "Lazarus" (for a time) because I had so many sores from falling. Now, Lazarus was a bible character who had acquired many sores on his body. Apparently, they were so bad he needed a physician to care for them. However, he couldn't afford a doctor's care, so the dogs would lick them instead. I trust his pain was not as severe as my own. I still remember my mom pouring alcohol on my cuts and abrasions while someone had to hold me down. The tears I shed under those circumstances should be a no-brainer.

I THOUGHT AS A CHILD

Nevertheless, my mom tried to console me by asking me "Why do you keep playing when you know you are only going to fall down?" She shared with me, that as a child she never learned how to ride a bike or to take on any kind of physical activity because she was always afraid of hurting herself. She just could not understand why, I was SO DIFFERENT. I later learned she always had a weak knee, which would give out under her. That is why she did not attempt to do anything physical. Although she may not have understood this as a child, she did know she HATED to fall and hurt herself. I, too, learned…later in my life that I had weak ankles. Hence, the reason that today if I am not careful or if I find myself walking on an unfamiliar walkway, my ankles may give out under me at any given moment, causing me to fall.

I UNDERSTOOD AS A CHILD

However, most of the time I was called Epaminondas (E-pa-min-non-das), a fictional character who provoked his mother to say; "I don't think you were born with any sense." When his mother would ask him to do anything, he would always do it the wrong way. Eventually she would say, "Now, I know you were not born with any sense."   My parents would always discuss this character in my presence as if I were invisible. 'Why did she do it this away or that way?' 'What is wrong with her?' 'She is just like Epanonis'.   I became their Epaminondas; no matter what I did, like him, I would do it all wrong.   I was backwards just like him; and they often reminded me of that.

[Since living in Detroit, I took it upon myself to locate this book in the public library. *I felt to read the book would help me better understand that I was not just dreaming this character up.* My cousin helped me with the pronunciation because my parents never pronounced his name right.   They called him "Epi-non-is."   I learned that Epaminondas was actually a part of my parents reading curriculum when they were in elementary school; that is how they became so familiar with him.

After getting the book and reading about him, I better understand who he was. However, I never understood how I became him.   This is one of the reasons I always felt like saying, "Excuse me for being alive; I apologize for still being here."]   It was definitely a family thing because that is where it all started; and family plays a hell of a part in our upbringing.

THEY SAW A CHARACTER FLAW

What is amazing to me, (then and now) is that I loved my family so much. What is more amazing is that it was my mother and my oldest sister that I loved, respected, and admired the more. [Actually, when I say family, I usually mean MY MOM AND/OR MY SISTER. They not only were in agreement on most things concerning me, they worked together in doing whatever was done in regards to me. I guess I gave them permission to do what they did because I adored them so.]

They took my compliancy for a weakness in my character. *I tried not to talk back or to make anyone angry. I tried exceptionally hard to please them. I tried so hard to do just as I was told. But, I believe my father, mother and my sister could not see me as a compliant child;* but rather as a complacent child. *They saw me wholly incapable of doing anything for myself.*

Moreover, I was scared to death of my dad and just stayed out of his way. But, I placed my mother on a pedestal because I believed her love for God was real; her faith in Him was solid as a rock. I placed my sister on a pedestal because I wished many days I could just turn into her, from the top of my head to the soles of my feet. As I have said earlier, she is

12 years older than I and never lived with us long enough for me to really get to know her. All I remember is, seeing her leaving the house and going off to school and soon after that, getting married. But while she was at home, I paid as much attention to her as I could. That is why I remember very well the first day I started school.

SHE WAS MY INSPIRATION

My sister was in high school and she was always carrying stacks of books to school. So naturally, I believed my first day of school meant I had to do the same. Right before my mom and I left the house to enroll me into kindergarten, I had a stack of heavy books in my small arms. My mother told me I did not need to take any books. I tried to convince her I had to take them with me; somewhat recognizing I had no hope of changing her mind. *I think I cried all the way to school because she just didn't understand.*

When we arrived at school, I tried to explain to the teacher through tear-stained eyes how I attempted to bring my books with me, but my mother would not let me. The teacher tried to resolve this matter as compassionate as one can to an unhappy 5-year-old child. When she said I did not need books in kindergarten, I began to look at her suspiciously. She tried to illustrate how busy I will be without them. That's when I discovered the toys and other activities which were at my disposal, and THAT evidently stopped my tears. I said all this because I had observed my sister and believed I had to do what SHE was doing. Even at the tender age of 5, I was hopelessly inspired by her. I wanted so much—to be just like her.

NOT QUITE GOOD ENOUGH

Moreover, my mother never had a problem telling me everything I needed to *know about her eldest daughter. Her first child was her pride and joy; with an intelligence beyond her years. My mom always reminded me how smart my sister was at my age. Because she could be trusted, she had the privilege of running all kinds of errands for the family; including important ones like taking public transportation downtown to pay the bills. My mother adored her so much. I guess this is why I thought so well of my sister. I wanted to walk like her and talk like her. I even wanted to be short like her, but my height soon dispelled that thought as I continued to grow.*

After my sister married and moved out of our home, my mom would reminisce on the pride she had in my sister. I would ask her over and over again to give me a chance to do some of the things my sister had been so good at. She would always tell me she could not trust me like she trusted my sister. She was the bright one. I could never be like her nor could I do what only she had been capable of doing.

I may have been wrong, but I felt when one sibling left the nest, then the next sibling in line would get the responsibilities and the same privileges of the one who left. I guess that was presumptuous of me. Never was I given a position similar to the eldest child in my home. I was pretty much treated like my younger sister with little difference made between the both of us. Moreover, I never hated my older sister; I just wanted to prove to my mother I was smart, too. But I learned that my older sister was my mother's favorite. Like my father, my mom had a right to have a favorite too.

As I moved into my teens, my mom had a growing concern about who I dated. She criticized most guys I dated, especially if they were too dark in complexion. What can I say? I had a natural attraction to guys who were darker than me. Like I said, I couldn't seem to do anything right and perhaps this is why my mom and my sister started making decisions for me, whether I liked it or not. For instance, both of them made sure I went to my senior prom, choosing the date for me, my clothes and everything. The problem was I did not want to go—but they made me. My prom date was not a bad guy, just the brother of the guy I really was in love with. THAT is too long of a story to comment on right now; but let me just say my prom was not a moment I wanted to cherish.

When I prepared to pledge myself to the future father of my children, my sister chose the wedding dress, the veil and all of the other particulars. I really don't remember having any say so in some of the most important events of my life. I had dated my children's father a few times and even accepted his proposal of marriage. However, as the day of the wedding drew closer, I began having second thoughts about this future father of my children. I felt in my heart that something was not quite right about him. I did have the courage to confide in my mother because it seemed everyone was excited about him and I joining in holy matrimony but me. It was more than just cold feet and I told her and not my father I did not want to go through with this marriage.

My mother looked at me and reminded me of all the gifts I had already received. Did I really expect her to give them all back? Did I expect her to call all her relatives who were coming from out of town and tell them the wedding was cancelled? Did I really expect her to call this whole thing off? She threatened me by saying I would be a disgrace to the family if I chose to back out of the marriage. Not only would I look bad, she too would be an embarrassment to the church, her neighborhood and to her family. She would have none of that. I was going through with this. *I was so determined to please her; I married him and literally forgot who had advised me to do it. [It took me more than 15 years to remember who had told me to marry him. I couldn't for the life of me recall who had given me such bad advice. Sometime after my divorce, I happened to be with my mother and simply told her I had been trying to recollect who exactly had told me I had to go through with my marriage. I knew it was someone I admired and respected but I hadn't been able to identify that person. She calmly said she was the one. I was simply dumbfounded: you cannot image my surprise. When it came to forgetting some things, I was becoming a MASTER at it!]*

I did not like what was happening to me. However, in spite of everything, I adored them both. It is because I loved them so much that I trusted them so. Have you ever loved someone so much that you let them define the very core of who you are? *I certainly hope not!* I actually allowed them to do this to me. Isn't that INCREDIBLE?   I was beginning to believe I WAS incapable of making decisions for myself.

A GROWING NEED—TO BE SET FREE

Somewhere, when I was well into my teens, I noticed there was something growing within my heart. *It would sometimes scare me because I felt something or someone else was there inside of me—trying to come out or break free.* When I shared this with my mother, (HEY, what can I say, she was my confidant) she told me it was only the devil inside of me. *It was my responsibility to keep it down there. Apparently, it was safer for me to keep it inside me than to let it come out.* She would then pray for me that the devil would not come out, overtake me and/or destroy me.

[I now realize that it was ONLY MY INDIVIDUALITY that longed to be set free. THAT EVIL *was ONLY my own hopes, dreams, creativity, and my own thoughts that WISHED to live and flow freely. I had a longing to be respected and to be embraced for who I really was.   I did not know I had to respect and embrace myself first and demand the same from others.]*

Moreover, self-love was practically nonexistent for me, *but my struggle to keep this evil in me from coming out was misconstrued, holding at bay the woman I needed to become. I did not realize the detriment I was causing myself, in not making that choice. It seemed apparent to me that n*o one around me could see my worth—if they did, I do not remember them telling me. Maybe everyone else were having their own struggle. So, I was pretty much on my own to figure it out as best I could.

This struggle within me was so real I began to believe something, indeed, was wrong with me. The questions I did ask and the comments I did make in my own defense were ignored, leaving me to feel SO DIFFERENT and my humanity unimportant. I felt as if I was not all there; *perhaps I was "CRAZY,"* as it has been inferred all of my life. Maybe God left something out of me, that others like my mother and my sister had.

I MEANT RIGHT IN MY HEART

I was about 16 when I started thinking seriously about God's will and purpose for my life. I knew he was real. I knew that people who loved Him suffered many things for His Sake. The Christian movies that I saw at that time depicted Christians humbly suffering and dying for their belief. They were beaten, cast into the lion den, hung, torn apart and killed because of their faith in God. I felt a kind of kinship with them and often I was crying harder for them than they were crying for themselves in the movies. *I felt destined to follow Christ because I felt just as misunderstood and very much like a throw away. I was someone people did not care to be around, and I didn't know why.*

My younger sister had more friends than I did. (That is funny because she could care less about them). But when it came to having friends, they were there for her [and they still are]. I, on the other hand, loved people. However, the harder I loved them, the fewer friends I had [and still do]. *Moreover, I felt I had all the signs and makings of a Christian (despised and rejected). I had only to commit myself to Him. So, I surmised that all of my suffering (in my family) was directing my life to follow Christ.* I would not be alone anymore. My mother would be there for me because she was the epitome of sainthood. Too me she was undoubtedly, a perfect example of a believer.

I mean she was actually trying to do what the Bible said, loving her enemy (my father) even when he said terrible things about her. Did it not say, rejoice and be exceedingly glad? (I am still paraphrasing here, for she was happily humming her songs in our home.) I just felt so rejected in my young life that I wanted some kind of happiness while living in this world too. She looked happy to me. So, I wanted what she had.

I always knew there was a God. Even when I doubted, I knew He was real. In my young life, I could see evidence of His kindnesses and of His faithfulness. Had I been called to this higher calling? *For better or for worse, I finally made the decision that my lifetime of suffering hinged on my need to be a part of those who found hope in…*

. . .

Suffering For Righteousness' Sake

(In The Name Of Jesus?)

CHAPTER 4

The bible says to rightly divide the word of truth. I believe The Word of God will set you free or keep you bound—it all depends on how you look at it. For years I thought I was interpreting it right, but it is now evident to me that I was not. You can use it to justify anything that you do in this flesh, be it right or wrong. The centuries of holy wars and devastations in the earth attest to this fact. When it is interpreted correctly, it brings life...when it is misinterpreted, it can bring death.

— My Personal Reflection

I grew up in a sanctified church—the Apostolic Faith—and we believed that Jesus was God in the flesh. My mother was saved, but my father was a backslider—one who once confessed the faith, but later left it. At seventeen years old my heart was so overwhelmed with the cares of this life. I did not feel like I BELONGED in school. In the Chicago Public School system, I was accidentally placed in an Essential grade level in the ninth grade. I did not have the full range of class choices most students had because I had been declared unable to read on a 6th grade level (I had just finished reading the novel "Gone With the Wind") —based on a high school entrance examination I took in the 8th grade. I was sick the day of the test and unable to finish it—and my parents later refused to contest the decision. That affected my four year matriculation through high school—something that should never occurred—because I knew I was better than that.

At home, I was so different from everyone else in my family, and I was often reminded of that. I was truly tired of being told that I was a failure at everything I tried.

IT WAS A PERSONAL THING TO ME

So, the day I gave my life to God, I received a ray of hope that my heart had never experienced. As I stood before my pastor, after the altar call on that Sunday morning, I felt something moving over me from the soles of my feet to the top of my head. I had never felt the movement of the Spirit. But on that day, as the Spirit of the Lord moved upon me, a continuous stream of tears fell down my cheeks. Every heartache, every disappointment, and every sorrow I had ever known was lifted from me. The concerns I carried were gone and the sweet relief I felt was so wonderful. I could not find the words to explain how grateful I was to God for what He alone had done; all I could say (over and over again) was, "Thank you Jesus!" For the first time in my life I felt totally free. This was not man's doing, but God's.

But, yet, I was still conscious of my pastor holding me and hearing him ask the congregation whether I had already been baptized. I was so humbled when I looked up at his face and said "No, sir, never." He wrapped his arms around me again and told the mothers to take "this child and prepare her for water baptism."

My tears were not of sorrow but of joy, as they dressed me and walked me to the waiting baptismal pool. I was immersed into the water in the Name of Jesus and escorted back into the dressing or/Mothers' room. That day would always hold a special place in my heart; a powerful demonstration of God's love for me. Simply put, I knew beyond a shadow of a doubt how real God was because I could actually feel his presence. Everyone who knows the Lord on a personal level know exactly what I am saying. Each of us have our own testimony. This was (and still is) mine.

When I turned 18, I began praying and seeking for the very spirit of God to dwell in me.

I realized, with the passing of time that feeling of serenity would not last always, because I lived in a world filled with upheaval. I had to go home some time. I had to deal with school and other things at some point. You see, my old ways of thinking were coming back. I needed to know what I could do to retain the glorious feeling I experienced upon my conversion. "What you are missing," one of our church mothers told me, "was the (filling of or infilling of) Holy Ghost."

Some believers are taught that conversion and the indwelling of the Spirit is one of the same or that they receive the Spirit of God in them at the same time they repent. Most churches believe in repentance and their life being changed—but we believed it went a step further. We believed in the Pentecostal experience. When the disciples of Jesus were in the upper room waiting for the promise of the Comforter, (which is the Holy Ghost or the Spirit of God) the Spirit actually came (like the sound a mighty blowing wind), it (appeared as a flame of fire) sat upon each of them and they began to speak in tongues (Acts 3:32).

This does not mean if you do not speak in tongues, you are not saved. Or, that you do not know the Lord or do not have the Lord in your life. It is a teaching we were given (I was brought up in) and I needed to know for myself, what was meant by "being filled with the Holy Ghost." I was not interested in hearing what everyone else thought because it was too personal for me to play with. When I spoke in that heavenly language, I received an assurance that He was not only with me but in me. I knew then, that He was able to keep me as I walked with Him from day to day. At that moment, I felt a type of completion in Him (unlike anything I would ever experience again).

MY FATHER IN THE LORD

My pastor was a Bishop, and he was a good man. I looked at him as my father in the Lord, the man in my life who loved God AND me. It was the kind of relationship my own father and I never had. I could talk to my pastor and I talked to him whenever I could. The church organization I grew up in was much younger than some of the other organizations around at that time like the Churches of God in Christ (COGIC) and the Pentecostal Assemblies of the World (PAW).

Fully rooted in the Apostolic doctrine, I believe Jesus Christ himself was the chief cornerstone of my faith. It remains today, the foundation of my teaching and MY PERSONAL

CONVICTION in regards to holiness.   I was raised in a bible believing, foot stumping, and tongue talking church that believed in having testimony services. [In those days most churches in the Apostolic churches conducted testimony service. Today, some do and some don't.   But, I must admit that I miss those declarations of God's goodness.]   In those services, members were given a space of time to tell the congregation about what God was doing in their lives. Those testimony services were precious to me and helped to keep me (and other believers) encouraged in my daily walk with God. Each testimony reminded me of God's faithfulness. Hearing what he was doing in the lives of others helped me understand God did not have a respect of persons.

COMING BACK TO BITE ME

Once I was filled, it did appear (for a time) I hadn't a problem in the world. Although the Lord had done a miraculous work in my life, there was something else that eventually reared its ugly head again. My sense of worthlessness was coming back. I have to admit, my fiancée saw to that. I met him after my encounter with Jesus. He said he had been born again too. But, I would soon discover his encounter with salvation and my encounter with salvation were two horses of a different color.

My fiancée had studied me and knew me better than I knew myself. He made sure my worthlessness stayed at an all-time low. My self esteem was the part of me I never acknowledged as a problem because—IT STILL APPEARED NORMAL TO ME. I was unconsciously taking it into my soon-to-be marriage.

It is like this: first of all, I did not know anything about verbal abuse. Second, once the verbal assaults (casual and infrequent as they were) started coming from my fiancée, I felt something was wrong with him but, at the same time, I was told by him something was wrong/off with me. That is why although I was saved and loving God all I knew how, I began to feel incomplete again, and the second reason I could not put my finger on it.

I did not ask God to improve my self-esteem. Heck, I did not know anything about SELF-ESTEEM—nor did anyone else in my circle of acquaintances. I don't remember anyone teaching about it, nor did I know any*one who actually prayed that prayer.* Actually, when you are first saved, your self-esteem is up. Salvation is what God does for you, making you over again as a new creature in Him, reconciling you back to Himself. And His system of deliverance is non stop. But we live in a world that is—what it is. Reality sets in when you least expect it and that includes bad feelings about your self. For me, words had almost destroyed me and I did not even know it.

After I married, I wondered when does an angel come down and make my partner do the right thing. When was God going to come down and make this man stop cursing me out. When was God going to make him stop fighting me. [Beloved, I had to learn it does not happen like that. *That's because as much as we want to make it spiritual, w*hen it comes to relationships you just need to make sure you are respected from the beginning—and that is not spiritual but natural.] I had a warped idea that my comfort and my feelings were not important and I did not interpret life correctly. I began to misconstrue who God was, my purpose was, my marriage was suppose to be and everything in between. To put it plainly, my interpretation of everything in my life and in the Christian world was tainted because I did not know HOW to RESPECT myself.

IS IT IN THE WORD?

Sometimes, I think there ought to be a WARNING SIGN on the cover of the Bible.

Warning: to misconstrue the Word of God is to commit spiritual suicide. You see, I was taught to love God's Word (the bible).   I was also told what ever I needed to know was in it.   If I needed wisdom or understanding, it was there. We believed the Bible was the infallible Word of God. That is why we were taught it had the answer regardless to what were going through— and to pray over everything. Unbeknown to me I began making every problem a spiritual one— needing God's intervention.

[I have now walked with the Lord for about 41 years.   I truly understand what it means when the bible says "Study to show thyself approved unto God, a workman that need not be ashamed, rightly dividing the word of truth," II Timothy 2:15.   It means when reading the Bible; you must read with an understanding. We use the Word like we would use a weapon, to protect and/or defend ourselves. But if we apply the Word to a situation inappropriately, we may do more harm to ourselves than good. Putting our heads through a spiritual noose can prove detrimental to our health as well as our faith.   That is what I nearly did.]

Before I entered my marriage, I started feeling bad about myself. My feelings of worthlessness continued after the vows were said. Left with very little trust in myself and being told I had no choices, I mistakenly used the bible to justify the situation I found myself in. It was as if the Lord was speaking to me from the Word, through the books I read, and the songs I sang; "Yes daughter, you must take it, the verbal abuse and the physical abuse as well."

My misinterpretation of God's Word kinda went like this. I Corinthians 10: 13, tells us "... he will with the temptation also make a way to escape, that ye may be able to bear it." I literally thought it meant God would provide me comfort, so I can continue to PUT UP WITH the ABUSE. St. Matthew 15:44 said "...love your enemies, bless them that curse you, do good to them that hate you, and pray for them which despitefully use you and persecute you...."

I would stand there and take the verbal abuse from my husband and then figure out a way to show my love to him. He treated me like a slave and I treated him like a King. And of course I would pray for him, in spite of what he did. Let me give you another example.

Luke 6:31-33, reads "...For if ye love them which love you, what thank have ye? For sinners also love those that love them. And if ye do good to them which do good to you, what thank have ye? For sinners also do the same." *I wanted to go beyond what a sinner did. I wanted desperately to be an example of the believers to the point of nearly destroying myself. But how do I love someone else, like I did myself, if I did not love me? And where does reciprocity come into play after me loving you with all my heart and soul?*

[Today, I am constantly asking the Lord to help me to love myself. I know he loves me genuinely, *but I still need His guidance— because I never learned how to love me. I know I should know how, but I never was told directly or indirectly how to do that. And God has shown great patience with me and is still teaching me how to love myself; the good AND the bad parts of me.]*

Peter asked Jesus, "...How oft shall my brother sin against me, and I forgive him? Till seven times? Jesus saith unto him, I say not unto thee, until seven times: but, until seventy times seven..."   St. Matthew 18: 21-22. *Forgiveness for me was unending. No matter what was done to me, I was always trying to forgive just like the Bible said. But even when a righteous effort is put forth to do what we perceive to be right, we still must not literally sacrifice ourselves to the point of our own demise.*

[When we do not use good judgment, we put ourselves in danger of losing our health, our spirit, our minds, our better judgment and our common sense—if we do not PAY close attention. We begin saying "I deserve to be cursed out." "I deserved that slap"; forgetting or not considering ABUSE IS NEVER JUSTIFIABLE!!!] My nephew told me once, "…you are taking the Bible literal." And I was. It was getting hard to turn the other cheek every time my husband slapped me—verbally and physically. And it was not getting easier.

The Word of God is supposed to give LIFE, not take it. Misinterpreting it was killing me. This also applies to some religious books I read. Authors can use scriptures to back up every word in their books. Sometimes they condoned ABUSE IN THE HOME. In my opinion, a prime example is the Doctrine of Submission—a very prevalent teaching at this place in time. In the doctrine of submission, the man is the head and the final authority and the woman is to submit to him like she would to God—in totally obedience. I do not mind telling you I have a serious problem with this.

The reason I feel this way is because whenever we deal with the will of a man, we are dealing with our flesh. God has a will and the flesh has a will as well and almost as powerful. Permitting anyone to have total obedience over another person can lead to a form of slavery. In other words, there is no compromise, there is no negotiation, there is no thinking going on only a slave-like submission to someone else. Isn't this what the slave traders and the slave owners practiced back in the day? You dressed like you were told or with what you were given; you eat what was given to you; you did as you were told. And those who were in control used the bible to justify this submissiveness (here we go again).   In 2009, this is still being taught in churches using God as the one who ordered this train of thought.

Had I followed such teaching to the "T" in my home, there is no limit to what my husband would have made me do because man (our outward man, the flesh we live in) tends to do what the flesh wants; anything and everything. He drank, smoked (whatever) and wanted to try every pornographic idea that the imagination could conceive. Now you go figure. I have seen women in the church so caught up in their men that they actually lost their minds trying to please them. They were unable to think straight anymore (for themselves). Our total confidence is supposed to be in God and not man. Our bodies and minds are the temple of God and we have to take care of both of them. You can't do that if your mind is gone.

I have spoken to some women and they said they had no problem with submitting to their husbands—their men were saved and living righteously. A dear woman in the church once told me that saved men were saved from the top of their heads down to their belly buttons—after that they are all men (with desires just like every other man). To each her own, and if that is what floats your boat so be it. However, I am only reminding you that WE DO HAVE CHOICES. Every man—or woman—has be persuaded in their own minds. ENOUGH OF THAT! Not only did I take the Word of God (and other reading materials) incorrectly, but I misinterpreted spiritual songs I listened to.

...COMPASSED ABOUT WITH SONGS OF DELIVERANCE

The whole time I was married, gospel music had always been my music of choice. Even before my marriage, rhythm and blues and gospel music was always an intricate part of my life. It took little effort for me to play gospel songs around my house, because I believed the Bible when it said "Thou art my hiding place; thou shall preserve me from trouble; thou shall compass me about with songs of deliverance...." (Psalms 32:7) That is exactly what I thought I was doing, surrounding my self with "songs of deliverance." In a state of fear, it made good sense to me to make my life as bearable as I could. Whether it was through a book, through a sermon, through a song; it did not matter, I had to find a way to endure it—to comfort myself.

I would take songs like "BE GRATEFUL" (a lovely song by the Hawkins Family) that made me think, maybe I should be grateful for everything, because life would never be perfect. As a matter of fact, after hearing the song several times, my ex would tell me, "Someone else WOULD LOVE to be in YOUR shoes." He would then try to preach/inform me that "any woman would love to have what YOU have. You have a man who is working his ass off to provide an ungrateful woman, with a house with a beautiful yard and garage, two beautiful children, a cat and a dog. What are you complaining about????"

He knew I was unhappy and he thought I should believe the song and get with his program. God knew the song did not promote abuse—but with a little encouragement from my ex, I took it to mean just that. Is there any wonder, I stopped playing the song in (and out) of his presence?

Another song I used to comfort me was "I WON'T COMPLAIN, GOD'S BEEN GOOD TO ME." When I first heard this song, I was present to hear the artist, James Lennox, sing it at a tiny church in Chicago before it became popular. It is where I bought my first tape of it. I pondered over it for some time and felt God was trying to tell me my good days really did out way my bad days, so I shouldn't complain. So, my ultimate goal was to stop complaining. That is what I felt. Again, let me emphasize the song did not say, ACCEPT THE ABUSE but I INTERPRETED IT THAT WAY, because my pain was so great and I accepted the song as my answer—to ENDURE IT.

[In actuality, I did not use those songs as songs of deliverance. I used them for SONGS of COMFORT. Comfort means *to soothe in time of grief or fear; console; to ease physically; relieve.* DELIVERANCE WAS NEVER IN THE MIX. Deliver means *to release or rescue; set free.* (It is) t*he condition of being delivered, esp. rescue from bondage or danger. I only sought comfort. I did not know I had a right to*

be set free, nor did I know HOW to be set free.
I HOPE YOU GET MY DRIFT HERE.]

I believe there are women who love God and are in an abusive relationship who will—MARK MY WORDS—use SIMILIAR songs as an encouragement to stay in a abusive lifestyle. That is an outrage, but God is my judge, I believe it is true.

JESUS NEVER SAID A MUMBLING WORD!

I am a firm believer that I am supposed to take His (Jesus') yoke upon me and learn of Him. That means understanding how he handled Himself when he walked the earth. And don't you dare say He never said a mumbling word when He was here. Jesus ALWAYS spoke up for himself and for others. He did not have to fight them because He spoke truth and mesmerized, or confounded THEM ALL. Sometimes he questioned them in return. He left them wondering or amazed, but never WAS HE SPEECHLESS; except maybe once, before Herod. This has led me to believe speaking up is a privilege and not a curse as I have been led to believe.

[You do not need salvation; have to speak in tongues; or pray until beads of sweat fall from your head, in order to get out of an abusive relationship. Either you speak up and make him/her stop it or leave him/her there.   My uncle used to tell me, when your significant other calls you out of your name, check him. Tell him not to call you that name again. If he calls you a name again, get out of that person's face because he/she does not respect you or your feelings and never will—they will continue to call you out of your name whether you like it or not.   In other words, it is then your call, YOUR decision to find the strength within you to stop it or keep on walking and not look back. If he apologizes and never does it again, then that means that he has respect for you and your feelings.]

ORDINARY PEOPLE

Even though we are believers, we hurt like everyone else. Why do we believe we are an exception to the rule OF SELF PRESERVATION, I will never know. The truth of the matter is words hurt no matter how many times you may say it doesn't and you are lying if you say verbal abuse is an ok part of life. It becomes a double lie when we are told we are pleasing God when we TAKE it. There are so many women (and some men), who are being verbally abused and are members of SOMEBODY'S church. I DON'T NEED STATISTICS, I WAS A STATISTIC.

I know from experience that it wasn't (and still isn't) an important issue in some churches today. Let me get away from the spiritual and talk from a natural point of view. Jesus taught in parables because it was hard for the people to understand the spiritual things he taught; but when he spoke about natural things they acquired a better understanding of what He meant (Matthew 13:10-36).

BEHOLD THE ROACH!

What I like about a cockroach is when you study it out, you will discover when its life is threatened; it will take wings and fly if it has to. This is a fact because I saw one do it. IF A COCKROACH WILL FLEE WHEN ITS LIFE IS UNDER ATTTACK, WHY DO WE SIT AND ALLOW SOMEONE TO ATTACT US WITH VERBAL ASSAULTS? IT WILL NOT STOP, IF YOU DO NOT STOP IT!!!

I believe there is also a similarity between verbal abuse and cockroaches. NOW, PAY ATTENTION! *The cockroach has been around a long time and is known for its resiliency. It may not be attractive or one of the creatures you would like to have for a pet, but its instincts will help it to survive. It can crawl through most openings and it multiplies at a rapid rate. It* doesn't matter about your economic level, (nor does it care what you may think), if it is permitted to live at your house and multiply, you can be sure it will take over.

Now let's look at verbal abuse. It too, has been around for a long time. It can be in a home for generations and the perpetuator is known for his/her resiliency because that is how it survives. It is not attractive, especially if it is being used against you or a loved one. It is found in every economic level and it doesn't care what you think. It generally eases into your life undetected (undercover or possibly ignored) but when it escalates, it does so very quickly because the abuser wants the power over you. If you do not stop it when you first see it, the incidents will quickly multiply and before you know it, it takes over.

It has taken 50+ years for me to understand that I am worth much more. However, I know there is an exception to every rule; but this is my opinion

THE TRUTH OF THE MATTER

One of the problems I have had with being a believer is hearing how I must be "willing to give up the right for the wrong," and/or "giving people the benefit of the doubt." Both are *sayings, I have heard throughout my lifetime and they seem innocent enough. The problem is people who hurt us verbally (especially on a consistent basis) do not need to be given any benefit. They need to be given truth. You are not doing them any good keeping your hurt to yourself and you are certainly not helping your mental or physical well-being either. You have to speak your convictions and tell them they are wrong.* Tell them the truth and let the chips fall where they may.

I am still learning how and when to speak up. Most of the time I do but sometimes I do not. But I am getting much better and for this I am eternally grateful. In my heart I was determined not to hurt anyone as I have been hurt. But I do not live a world where people think like that. I live in a world where everyone wants to get their point across one way or another. Since my opinion IS AS important as yours, I am striving to BE TRUE TO MYSELF BY KEEPING IT REAL.

IT WAS A CONFUSING THING

I knew Jesus for myself, but I was seeing this spiritual thing all BACKWARDS. *After so many years, my impression of God had actually changed for the worse. I did not see him as the loving Father he was, but as the Test Examiner. I believed that the Lord was directing my children's father to perfect my walk with God, so I had to tolerate the abuse from him. My ability to withstand would prove my faith in God or help me to pass THE TEST.*

BEHOLD THE TEST!

I was the believer; my husband was the unbeliever. My TEST was based on my ability to demonstrate a Christ-like demeanor in every area of my life, especially in my home. If I tried to run from my bad marriage, I was avoiding the TEST. Moreover, THAT was an automatic failure—causing delay in the testing process. To divorce or sever myself from my husband meant I would be alone for the rest of my life—forfeiting ever marrying again. If I remarried, I would remarry in sin. Also, to remarry meant I would only find someone who was possibly worse—meaning I would have to retake THE TEST. But, my ex-husband could remarry because he wasn't saved; he wasn't a believer and free from condemnation. Hmmmmm!

How God assessed THE TEST, I am not sure, but here is what I surmised. If my children's father got saved, I passed. If he died while I was taking THE TEST, I would pass it. If I died while going through THE TEST, I probably passed—especially if the mental and physical assaults led to it. As a genuine martyr—I also would be heaven bound. The best of both worlds was that my husband surrenders his life to Christ; the abuse automatically stops because his new commitment to God would make him. Hmmm!

LAST, BUT NO WAY LEAST!

So many times I have heard over the pulpit and in the songs we sing, that "God will fix it;" "Hold your peace and let the Lord fight your battle;" and "This is a spiritual warfare, you cannot fight the enemy on a natural basis. Fight him with your praise." Most people, I believe, will take those words to mean, do nothing or praise Him in the midst of your trial and He will bless you. Just wait on God. Yes, there are some things only God can do. But, I have learned that there is a difference between a prayer meeting and a bear meeting. You pray in a prayer meeting; in a bear meeting you had better handle you business like that bear might kill you—nothing spiritual about a bear attacking you—and you better not get on your knees and start praying. Even when it comes to prayer we are exhorted to WATCH AND PRAY.

*Be aware, beloved, there are some things the Lord has put in you and me, which **you and I must do for ourselves.** I am also learning that the Lord does not have to DO EVERYTHING FOR me. I have the authority/the ability to stop THINGS THAT ARE detrimental to my health. I do not have to be ACCEPTING OF EVERYTHING THAT HAPPENS TO ME. I DO HAVE A SAY SO in some of these matters.*

Howbeit, verbal abuse is just that—ABUSE— and to justify it, make light of it and tolerate it is not acceptable. In the meantime, my mother said she never had a problem with people calling her out of her name. She even had a little jingle that went like this...

· · ·

Sticks and Stones May Break My Bones...
(But Words Can Never Hurt Me!???)

CHAPTER 5

I stand amazed as youth and adults alike take lightly the terrible words they call each other, especially in a love relationship. It appears to simply be a way of life. Then I have to remember what I went through in my childhood and my marriage. I did not know any other way of living existed—except on television (a long time ago). I want to reach out to those young people and to those adults and tell them you deserve better!

– My Personal Reflection

As I think on that jingle/phrase, I realize that my mother said many things that she herself may or may not have believed.

BACK IN THE DAY

When I was in elementary school, kids commonly called each other out of their names. [The difference between that day and this one is the name calling is of such that it has become a type of flattery. We have girls and women who believe their being called a "bitch" is actually a compliment. Back in the day, that name was a disgrace to most. Also, if someone was told to "KISS MY BUTTE" they would take offense, knowing that would never happen. Today, if someone says that, they just might get what they are asking for!]

I believe most all children have had to endure the name-calling ritual at some time in their lives. But what I realized as a child was that some kids COULD HANDLE IT and kept right on going. I, like so many others, did not know just how to respond to it. It was frustrating because I learned in sunday school to treat others the way I wanted to be treated, and if I became scared, then run. [It did not take me long to realize, that once you start running from people, you may be running for the rest of your life.]

So, I would come home disconcerted because some one had been bad mouthing me. Since my mom never saw me fighting, she would tell me to tell them (with tears whelming up in her eyes, just as if SHE was the victim), "Sticks and stones may break my bones, but words will never hurt me. You can talk about me, but you sure can't EAT ME!" Then she would say, "Tell them that!" I know she meant well, but those words did not make me feel better NOR did they ring true with me. [Today, I still say words hurt because I know what words can do. Pretending that words do not affect us is not a strength but a weakness... weakening our resolve, our uniqueness and our dreams.]

WORDS CAN KILL YOU!!

Words are why I never celebrated myself. I was raised in an atmosphere that contributed to the opposite; moreover, how could I accentuate what I could not see. Instead, I found just enough strength to put up with the insults I incurred during my lifetime.

Beloved, WORDS CAN KILL!!! Its destruction, when directed at you, will set you apart in a room full of people and strip you of your dignity and your self-worth. I knew what the tongue was capable of and I tried to be careful of what my tongue said because it truly is full of deadly poison (James 3:8). I was always cognizant of my hurting someone else because I sincerely tried to love everyone. However, I often did not think twice about how others spoke to me. Not that it didn't hurt, because it did; not that I didn't know I deserved the same respect, eventually I knew that too. But, I just did not know how to stop it or fix it in my own behalf.

THE ORIGIN OF THIS BOOK

This chapter is where this book originated. While I was sitting on my parent's front porch in Chicago, I could hear my father railing at my mother from within. She must have been babysitting that day because a whole host of children were in the front of the house playing. I think the group of children was made up of my nieces and nephews and great nieces and nephews (and possibly a young cousin here or there). I got a pad and started to write down all the names my mother had been called by my father through the years. I do not remember whether the children were outside because they were getting away from the ranting of their granddad or because he put them out. But, I know they were ignoring the drama within. I wanted to know their thoughts and I needed their input.

I pulled some of them together and I asked them to tell me all the names they heard their grandpa called their grandmother. They looked at me and laughed. "We can't say those bad words; we'd get in trouble." "Not, if I don't tell," I replied. Someone asked me why I needed to know this. I told them I was planning on writing a book. After a little more persuasion, they were more than happy to contribute. [And I never told on them, like I promised (smile!).]

I added a few more names I had been called by my father and by my children's father. Somehow, I believed this would be therapeutic for me. It was the first time I felt a reassurance that I was able to change the direction my life was headed in. [Never did I know just how much this book would mean to me as I strived to heal myself from the powerful programming I had been given.]

It was Dr. Maya Angelo who said, and I am paraphrasing again, "Words have a way of attaching themselves to your clothes, to the walls of your home, to the windows and doors of your house." I believed words can attach themselves to the physical structure of my home, I believe those words attached themselves to the recesses of my mind and to the depths of my heart. Those words began sculpting me when I was a child, moved with me into my marriage and have stayed with me long after my divorce was finalized. Since I did not know how to ignore, avoid, or destroy them; they attached themselves to me with the express intention of destroying my today and my tomorrow.

I CALL IT THE "KILLING FIELDS"

The "Killing Fields" were an intricate part of my upbringing. I call it that because it was a place where words were all around me, the white elephant, that everyone saw, but no one acknowledged it being there. A place where words were constantly thrown around to hurt and debilitate the recipient and no one had the nerve or knowledge to stop it. So rather than being a "A Field of Dreams", that place became a field where dreams were killed and marred.

My parental home was where I lived and breathed low self esteem because I was nurtured in the "Killing Fields". My marital home was merely a new location, where trust would never be evident, feelings of helplessness was encouraged, and deceit ran rampant. I was self-destructing in a household where there was no semblance of genuine love, trust, fairness, or hope. My innocent children would be nurtured by a mother who was afraid to speak up and a father who felt he was always right—therefore setting a pattern that would forever affect their lives.

My talented daughter would become the 4th generation of abused women in my family. She would continue the cycle she was bequeathed to live. In her search for love, she would find herself in abusive marriages and relationships that were a constant reminder that she would never be quite good enough. She would see the mental and physical abuse I tolerated from her dad and think it was NORMAL TO ENDURE IT until she too reached a breaking point, get away from it: then return to take some more.

I cringe when I think of some of the things she went through; some of the things she had to endure in her journey to and in womanhood. As a young mother, I could not help her avoid them, because my life was always in the survival mode—I could not even help myself. So her example of being a strong woman was practically none existent in our home. *[Today, I keep encouraging her when I can, to be stronger than I had been. I try to assist her in her discovery of the beautiful woman that is within her, by validating her uniqueness, guiding her kindnesses, and strengthening her greatness. Such conversations have assisted her in strengthening her own daughters—helping her to avoid making some of same errors I made in raising her.]*

My only son also saw the abuse his father used towards me. Although he is the oldest, he and I have not spoken to one another as often or to the same extent his sister and I have. As a matter of fact, he refuses to speak of what he saw in my marital home. I know he loved his dad because right or wrong, his dad was a powerful influence in his life. How does a mother tell her son, "your dad and I set a terrible example before you during a time when you needed a true outlook on life?"

How do I help him overcome the anger, the helplessness he must have felt, to see his mother being dragged through the house by his father? How do I say your dad was wrong and so was I? How do I tell you that slamming doors and cabinets, when angry, were not the correct way to handle anger? How do I explain what you called abandonment, was not an abandonment of you. I can only hope time and God will guide you—help you discover what REAL LOVE is all about. You were brought up in the "Killing Field" I helped to create, baby; and for this I apologize.

[Today, I do not know what a good man looks like. I know he is out there, but at times, I do not know if it is a camouflage I am looking at. How do I tell my son or daughter this? For it takes time to really get to know a person—looks and some quick responses, can never tell you what you need to know about their character. But, as I ponder over these things in my own mind, I do realize that loving one's self has to come

first. Until a woman loves and respects herself, she will never find and correctly cherish that other individual. Until she understands how she should be treated, she will never be able to share her likes and dislikes with him. Someone truly loving you hinges on how much you truly love yourself.]

Although, I did not ever call my children out of their names [one of my gifts to them], I nurtured them in an environment I did not know how to escape, a place that only grew deeper in despair with the passing of time.

So I present to you an opportunity to know me better. You do not know me if I never tell you who I am or what I think. I have taken the names that I and my mother have been called; and I will tell you what they meant to me and/or how they made me feel. It is a type of memorial I created to what I learned in the midst of the "Killing Fields; a few of the names I was called while there. A place I will never, ever return to in this life time.

Please do not take any offense because I make NO APOLOGIES.

"YOU ARE GOOD FOR NOTHING!" – There is nothing I am good for or good at. I will never be good for anything or good at anything, because I never will have any worth.

Part One—Trusting Others

"YOU ARE A GOOD FOR NOTHING BITCH!" – I am a female dog that will never be good for anything or good at anything, because I have no worth.

"YOU HAVE A SERIOUS PROBLEM!" – I must have a problem when it comes to thinking and doing things.   I require the abuser's assistance and at this time; ultimately, I am beyond his help. The bearer of the tidings does not have the same problem so he is obligated to show me and/or remind me of my inadequacy.

"YOU ARE DUMB!" – I am lacking the power of speech: mute, temporarily speechless with shock or fear. I am not capable of processing my own thoughts.

"YOU ARE A FOOL!" – I am incapable of helping myself. I am incapable of normal behavior.

"YOU ARE STUPID!" – I am slow to comprehend or just plain dumb. I show a lack of intelligence. I react as if I am in a daze or as if I am stunned. My life is pointless and of little worth to anyone, including myself.

"YOU ARE A STUPID-ASS!" - I am a person who does not have the intelligence of a stupid horse.

"YOU ARE A STUPID-ASS BITCH!" – I lack the intelligence of a stupid female dog and horse combined. I am not worth your trouble to get to know me and my existence is nonexistent for you.

"YOU ARE A SORRY EXCUSE FOR A WOMAN!" – When my womanhood is compared to other women, I am a disgrace. I am an embarrassment and do not deserve the place I am holding in your life as a woman or person.

"YOU ARE NO DAMN GOOD!" – I am eternally damned when it comes to my purpose on this earth. I am predestined to having no goodness or any ability to be worthwhile on this earth. My conception was not even a good thought

"YOU ARE FULL OF SHIT!" – I am so unproductive, I am unable to create, formulate or perform anything worth while or of value. That of which I do manage to produce is comparable only to horse manure, geese/bird droppings or the feces produced by human beings.

"YOU ARE A LAZY-ASS BITCH!" – I even lack the qualities of a stupid female dog and a horse combined. Any kind of labor is beyond me and therefore I am of little use to you.

"YOU ARE A GOOD-FOR-NOTHING WHORISH ASS BITCH!" – I will never be of value to you because there is nothing in me worth having around. I do not have the innate abilities to have a sexual encounter that is even comparable to a female dog and/or horse, I do not even do that well. Your exaggerated episodes of me cheating on you, leaves you to believe I am a hopeless slut, at best.

"YOU ARE A SANCTIFIED BITCH!" – I am a female dog that refuses to satisfy my spouse's sexual preferences, because it is against my religious conviction.

"YOU WILL NEVER BE ANY DAMN GOOD!" – I have no hope of acquiring any worth, qualities, or values that will satisfy another person.

"YOU ARE A HALF-WHITE ASS BITCH!" – I am a female dog whose skin color reflects both Caucasian and African ancestry that disgusts my spouse and is nasty to look at.

"YOU ARE A STUPID BALD-HEADED BITCH!" – I am a female dog who has lost some or most of my hair on my head; therefore, I am not a whole woman. I am too dumb to please a man.

"YOU ARE A STUPID ASS HOE!" – I am as dumb as a stupid mule/horse, who lacks the

ability to swap sexual favors; therefore, I am beneath a professional whore on the street.

"YOU ARE A FAT-ASS LYING BITCH!" – I am an overweight female dog, incapable of telling the truth, a hopeless example of woman who cannot be trusted.

"YOU ARE A CRAZY BITCH!" – I am equivalent to a female dog who just said something that surprised the originator of the term.

"YOU ARE A CRAZY-ASS BITCH!" – I am synonymous to a female dog that just did something that displeased or scared the originator of the term. The originator is also the recipient of the action.

"YOU AIN'T SHIT!" – I have proven that I am incapable of accomplishing anything worthwhile. Regardless of the achievements I have obtained, they are not worth mentioning because I am the one who did it. Ultimately, my character, dreams, beliefs, and my humanity are non existent. If I am anything, I am not as valuable as a pile of human excretion.

"YOU ARE A MOTHER FUCKING LIE!" – I am a person who has sexual intercourse with her maternal mother and I am totally incapable of telling the truth; unable to determine what is true or what is false, what is good or bad.

"YOU ARE A STANKY BITCH!" – I am a female dog who possesses a terrible body odor that is strong, continuous and annoys the originator of the term. Therefore, my presence is unappreciated, apprehensible and unwanted.

"YOU ARE A CROSS-EYED NIGGER!" – I am a lazy no good person who is unable to fix the eye I purposefully messed up. Therefore, someone must remind me of the error of my ways, so I will one day admit I did this to myself.

"YOU ARE A NO-GOOD, CROSSED-EYED YELLA NIGGA!" – I am all of the above and then some. I am of no worth because my skin color reminds you of a young baby's defecation, uniquely odd specimen, and odd member of the family, sticking out like a sore thumb, who does not belong. I am an outcast, black sheep, crossed eyed, ridiculous to look at, like the clown that I am.

"YOU ARE A CROSS-EYED, CLUMSY, YELLA-ASS NIGGAH!" – I am damned because I am all of the above, and then some. I cannot stand on my feet without falling. I should not do anything to hurt myself, but I do it all the time. What is wrong with me, scarring myself up like that? I deserve pity, and lots of it.

"YOU ARE NOTHING MORE THAN A DAMN LAZARUS!" – Why can't I stand up without falling? Why am I too stubborn to admit the truth? I am worse than Lazarus: at least he did not keep falling down. I am predestined to failure because I think I can do things, I can never do. I cannot do anything well and I have the scars to prove it. My relentless pursuits to accomplish things only make me look like I have absolutely no sense at all. I will always be a failure.

"YOU ARE JUST LIKE EPAMINONDAS!" – I cannot do anything right. Everything I attempt and everything I do is wrong. I do not know how to differentiate between right and wrong and I prove that on a daily basis. My case is hopeless and I was born without any sense. My parents are convinced of this. Now, I too should be convinced of this.... After all, they could not lie on me.

"YOU ARE A GOD-DAMN LIE!" – I am not only a liar, but my lying is totally unbelievable. I am supposed to be a saint and lying like that. I am damned to hell because of it. I have no idea what I am saying and God, Himself will vouch for a sinner like you against a believer like me. I am damned by God to hell and I have

nothing to stand on, for even the Word of God has condemned me.

"WHAT THE HELL IS WRONG WITH YOU?" – Where did you come from? You must have come from hell. No one on this earth acts like you do, talks like you do, unless they escaped from hell. You do not belong here.

"WHO DO YOU THINK YOU ARE?" – I am not all that, but I think I am. I look like everyone else, but I think I am somehow better. You are here to serve me notice. I am just like everyone else. That really is all. How dare I think that I am better than all the rest of you? How dare me!

LET'S KEEP IT REAL

Verbal abuse by any other name is still the tearing down of an individual's self-worth.   It is still unacceptable regardless from whom it originates. There is no justification for it. The results are the same when it goes unchecked. When perpetuated long enough, the damage is phenomenal and can last forever.

For me, a person of color, Racism (or White Supremacy) parallels verbal abuse within the Christian community. The similarities are very evident when we take a closer look.

African-Americans continue to wait for the oppressor to bring us total deliverance from the institutionalized system that created us. Christians are waiting for Jesus to bring them total deliverance from verbal abusive relationships. African-Americans continue to accept for the most part whatever our society deems acceptable. Christians continue to believe we are what the abuser calls us. African-Americans have not taken our education or progress to the next level (as a group), but continue to get further behind as a group economically. Christians spend a great part of their lives living with verbal abuse; and because of the mental torture, get farther behind in our mission, our ministry and our covenant because we are so mentally exhausted. Both African-Americans and Christians have had *mental breakdowns* simply trying to ENDURE.

My struggle with self worth has altered my hopes and my dreams—AND I BELIEVE IT WILL ALTER MY FUTRUE IF I DO NOT continually ACKNOWLEDGE ITS DESTRUCTIVNESS AND COMMIT MYSELF TO IRRADICATING ITS DEVASTATION in my life. WORDS CREATED THE LIFESTYLE—AND IT WILL TAKE WORDS THAT SAY AND MEAN THE TOTAL OPPOSITE to REVERSE ITS AFFECT.

Words that BUILD ME UP are as POWERFUL as Words THAT TARE ME DOWN. Words that ENCOURAGE ME are JUST AS POWERFUL as Words THAT DISCOURAGE ME. Surrounding myself with Words that HEAL and with people who care about me, will (with time) reverse the affect that DESTRUCTIVE WORDS and negative people HAVE created.

NOBODY KNOWS THE TROUBLE I'VE SEEN

I only needed to remove myself from the situation if I could not handle it. The Lord has always been with me, waiting for me to use the knowledge and understanding I did not believe I had. After I discovered and acknowledged the trouble I was in, I had to make a decision.

I could either stay in my marriage (stand up for myself—which meant I had to stop the verbal assaults on my life and the physical fights that resulted) or I could leave. After doing everything I could to keep my family together, it was ....

. . .

My Decision To Leave

(Look At The Hand—Trying My Best To Get Out Of Dodge!)

CHAPTER 6

Some say you have to get sick and tired of being sick and tired—tired of crying; tired of being afraid; tired of being hurt; tired of being ridiculed. I tried three times to leave, only to find myself returning. Now, if I trusted myself, my heart, & my God to go with me, I would not have gone through all that drama.

— My Personal Reflection

ATTEMPT NUMBER ONE

The first time I left him, I moved back in with my parents. It was around Christmas and I found work at a store in downtown Chicago. I stayed with them for about two weeks. My parents welcomed me back warmly. However, my dad's verbal attacks on my mom had escalated. Nevertheless, I felt more comfortable at my parents' home than I did in my own. [As I reflect on that moment, I wonder how I felt any kind of comfort. Perhaps it was because the verbal assaults were not directed at me, but rather at my mother. I actually believed it was a reprieve for me. Unconsciously, I was simply glad it was no longer me being verbally attacked.]

My pastor then summoned me to a counseling session. *My children's father had been calling me, apologizing for fighting me and trying to persuade me to come back home. It took all the strength I could muster to listen to these pleas and be strong enough to stand my ground. I told him, I forgave him but I was not coming back.* My "ex" was *learning when all else failed, going to my pastor, crying and confessing his sin would turn the situation in his favor.* I discovered HE WAS RIGHT. When I attended the session, my children's father was already there. When I entered his office, my pastor asked him to leave.

I was told my husband had repented for all the wrong he had done. *If I did not accept his apology: which meant to forgive him; which also meant going back to him, I would be the one in error.* In fact, I would be unable to pray anymore, because God would no longer hear my prayers. I went back to my husband because a man said I had to. [I NOW realize my response was one of total obedience to man and not God.] Moreover, I did not ask God anything because I was told that if I was disobedient to the man of God, I was disobedient to God. *Let me further explain…*

THIS BINDING THING

This scripture was often preached in Sunday morning services. "Jesus asked his disciples, Whom do men say that I the Son of Man am?" (Matthew 16:13). After a few responses Jesus asked them:

"But whom say ye that I am? And Simon Peter answered and said, Thou art the Christ, the Son of the living God." And Jesus answered and said unto him, "Blessed art thou, Simon Barjona: for flesh and blood hath not revealed it unto thee, but my Father which is in heaven.

And I say also unto thee, that thou art Peter, and upon this rock I will build my church; and the gates of hell shall not prevail against it.

And I will give unto thee the keys of the kingdom of heaven: and whatsoever thou shalt bind on earth shall be bound in heaven: and whatsoever thou shalt loose on earth shall be loosed in heaven." (Matthew 16:15-19)

I had been taught that Jesus had given the pastor the right to open and shut heaven. *If he petitions God not to accept my prayers, or bind heaven, God would do it, because he was the pastor. But, if the pastor would petition God to loose heaven or receive my prayers, his request would be honored. At that point God would hear my prayers. With all of that against me, I went back to the batterer because I did not feel God would even permit me in His presence. I actually believed His will for my life was to endure this suffering!*

[I am so glad that I know better now. It took me moving to Michigan, and sitting under some wise mothers to break it all down to me. All believers have that authority to bind and loose heaven. It was not only given to the pastor.] I also talked to another great Man of God and after I explained to him that type of teaching. He agreed and said, "Yes, we do teach that."

So, I politely told him, "That a woman in a similar situation is damned if she do and damned if she doesn't."

He laughed and said, "We are just men, Sister, and we can make mistakes."

I stuck an imaginary pin in that line (in the recesses of my mind) and told him, "God is going to get some men and women for speaking life and death into his people."

If we, the people of God, do not get to know our Lord and Savior on a very personal level, *we are susceptible to embracing what man and man alone, say.* I am not saying that a pastor cannot advise us on some matters. But, we had better be sure we can talk to God for ourselves. That is the REASON JESUS DIED FOR US, so we can have DIRECT ACCESS TO HIM.

[But I still stand behind my original thoughts about abuse. You do not have *to cry out to God, about whether or not you should run for your life and for the lives of your children.* Common sense should kick in and say GET THE HELL OUT OF DODGE. Then ask God to go with you and to go before you and HE WILL DO JUST THAT.]

ATTEMPT NUMBER TWO

The next time I left my children's father, my brother helped me and my children to move to Saginaw, Michigan, where most of my mother's family lived. I moved in with my mother's oldest brother, who was single at that time. I stayed with him for almost a month. My uncle welcomed me and my children when he found out I was getting away from an abusive situation. I enrolled my five year old son into kindergarten and my two year old daughter into Head start. I, in the meantime started looking for work.

I almost had a job at the post office (I later learned), when I got a long-distance call from my pastor. *He told me I could not run from God and my responsibilities. The children's father had approached him again and said he was sorry for what he had done and wanted me back. I was told it was my duty, as a saint of the most High God, to return to my home and make things right. I told him I would.*

When I hung up the telephone, I was more determined than ever NOT to return. Later, one of my dearest cousins (who was corresponding with my pastor at the time), an evangelist, called me and talked with me. She lived in Saginaw also and felt an obligation to counsel me in the WAYS OF GOD. *I must tell you, she was an evangelist among evangelists, and ran numerous revivals at my home church in Chicago. I admired her and loved her dearly.*

[I realize today that I don't need to worry so much about those who appear to be my adversary; I need to worry about those whom I love and admire so much. Those are the ones who have the ability to get very close to me and hurt me more!]

My Decision To Leave

She asked me whether I had talked to my pastor. I said "yes" I had. She asked me whether I promised my pastor I was going back home. I told her "yes". She asked me was I going back. I told her "No! I was tired of my husband's threats, his use of profanity and all the fights. I was staying here." *She told me, if I promised the Man of God I would return, then I had to keep my promise. To do anything less would prove me a liar and not a saint.*

It seemed as if I could not find a good reason to protect myself (although two children were reasons enough). Nor did I possess the self-esteem and strength to fight back. I did not see I had the right; I could not see I had a choice—I had a right to be free of a life that was detrimental to me and to my children. Instead, I felt trapped and did not know what was in my own best interest. I went out and bought a nice Christian book, which really encouraged submission to one's husband. I do not remember the title, but I remember the sadness I felt when I decided to go back home. I believe I cried all the way back to Chicago.

[It is imperative that you respect yourself and the voice that *you hear inside your own HEAD.* I could not hear me. My voice wasn't loud enough to drown out the voices around me.

I figured I just wasn't' spiritual enough. How could I BE RIGHT, and the men and women of God, I so highly respected, BE WRONG?]

ATTEMPT NUMBER THREE

When I left him the third time, I moved in with my oldest sister, who also resided in Chicago. Remember the one I adored—12 years older than me—the one I wish I could be like. She was already into her second marriage, had married her childhood sweetheart and appeared to be quite happy. She had nine children from her first marriage and acquired three more from her husband's previous marriage. I believe the last four or five of the nine were still with her at the time.   The others had attended college, (if they chose to) had families of their own and were doing well for themselves. I couldn't have been prouder of these nieces and nephews' accomplishments, if they had been my own. My children and I lived with them for most of that summer.

MUCH NEEDED INTERVENTION

My social worker suggested we get family counseling. But that didn't work because the children's father (enraged because I had left him again) did not believe he had a problem, so he refused to attend the sessions. I was enrolled in a program for battered women, in particular, spousal abuse. That was a turning point in my life. There were other women in that support group who were in situations much like my own. Until then, I did not know that some wealthy and professional women were in the same boat. I heard things there I never would have otherwise heard or learned (in regards to verbal and physical abuse).

I even met a woman who was in the same kind of church I was in. She and I spent countless sessions trying to explain to the group why we could not divorce our abusers. We kept telling them how our walk with God kept us in our relationships. I told them that if I divorced my husband, I had been told I would not be free to marry again. If my husband asked me for forgiveness the church said, I had to forgive him and at some point going back home, which was an act of faith. My adherence to the teachings of the church would put me in right standing with God. The support group leader never quite understood what we were saying, but we defended our stance until the end. I am certain she thought we were mentally deficient—but we HAD to be EXCELLENT examples of the abused women she met as an intervention counselor.

I THOUGHT IT WAS A SPIRITUAL THING

I felt anyone who was not in the sanctified church could never understand my perspective. Psalms 1:1 said, "Blessed is the man that walketh not in the counsel of the ungodly, nor stand in the way of sinners, or sitteth in the seat of the scornful." This meant any person (my counselor in particular) who is not in the faith, would not be able to really counsel me. They would only scoff at my belief and call me crazy for thinking like I did. "Do not seek them or follow after their ways." I just gave you a perfect example of that. That is why the two of us in those counseling sessions got along so well. We figured God had brought us together to comfort one another during this time in our lives.

[We were terribly mixed up; okie doked; on the wrong side of the tracks; bamboozled; on the deep end; in left field—and DID NOT EVEN KNOW IT. Yes, we were counseled and went right back to our husbands because we thought it was God's will for our lives. It seems so strange now, that I did this. No wonder I love God so much—he winked at my ignorance and realized I did not understand. The truth was, we did not want to live the rest of our lives ALL ALONE.]

A LIGHT AT THE END OF THE TUNNEL

There was, however, one thing that I did take back to my marriage. I REALIZED I did not have to take the physical abuse any more and I didn't. I knew I could stop the physical assaults by threatening to call the police—I told him so (and he actually believed I would). I had obtained the knowledge (thanks to that intervention counselor) and the strength to follow through. But, I did not know how to stop the verbal abuse, which kept coming all day, every day. The verbal abuse alone caused great fear and anxiety in me. His slamming doors and slamming cabinets kept me agitated. Throwing heavy objects on the floor, hitting the wall and the continuous threats, left me fearful of what was coming next.

We had a little dog tied up in the back yard. I cannot remember his name, but any time my children's father would get real angry at me, he would take a belt or a stick and go outside and beat that poor dog. I felt so sorry for it, but I realized that he was really BEATING ME.

Perhaps that should have given me some consolation, but it didn't. That dog would be yelping and I would be crying for him and for myself.

Now, you see why it was imperative for me to begin…

. . .

Checking Out!
(Running For My Life…)

CHAPTER 7

Starting over is not easy. Some of the hardest things I have done required me to find the courage and the strength from within to move forward with my life. That is no joke. But, I understood if I did not change my surroundings, I would be in the streets, in an insane asylum or dead. With those other choices, starting over did not seem so bad after all.

– My Personal Reflection

THE INTERPRETER

I was leaving my husband for the fourth time. When I requested this counseling session, it was with my pastor AND his wife. As I sat before them, I started to explain why I wanted out of this marriage. The verbal assaults had escalated, the mental cruelty (threats to kill me, threats to make me leave), the infidelity were non-stop. I would say a couple of sentences to my pastor and his wife would stop me. She would then explain to my pastor what I had just said.

He said "Whaaattt!"

Then I would describe something else. She would stop me and explain to the Man of God, what I had said.

His reply during the whole session was, "Whaaattt!"

She was interpreting everything I said! I never knew I needed an interpreter for all those years I talked with him. I thought he saw the tears and heard my pleas—only to discover on that day, he never heard one word I said! I was totally amazed.

FREE AT LAST!

When I finished talking, he looked at me and said, "Daughter, you are free. You were free a long time ago!" NOW *I was in total shock. Then I felt relieved. And then I was HAPPY TO FINALLY HEAR THAT WORD...FREE!* This is what I had waited all those years for. This is what I had longed for and trusted God for: The MAN OF GOD TO FREE ME! Then he added; if I was ready to start my life all over again without my husband "You have my blessing!" But, if I decided to give my marriage another try, I could do that too. At that point, on that day, I finally had an intelligent choice! What-do-you-think-I-did? Yes, Beloved, I took his blessing and went immediately to Legal Aide!

[It would take me years of looking back to realize that the journey I WAS ADVISED TO GO ON—WAS NOT EVEN NECESSARY! Every time I revisited THAT DAY; every time I thought about his telling me I "WAS-FREE-A-LONG-TIME-A-G-O," I would become so angry. I know I HAD TO GO ON WITH MY LIFE BUT it did something to my heart. I had tried to guard my heart; tried to do what I perceived was right; tried to love and forgive each and every day. But from that day forth I would NEVER be quite the same.

For, I had to admit, I had to recognize that, *if I had followed my own mind from day one…I would have not only left that marriage a long time ago, BUT STAYED AWAY! I REALIZED THE PAIN I FELT WAS REAL AND I DID NOT NEED ANY ONE TO VALIDATE THAT FOR ME. I DISCOVERED MY MIND WAS GOOD AND I WAS RIGHT ALL ALONE. And, THE PEOPLE I DECLARED HOLY, RIGHTEOUS AND THE EPITOMY OF PERFECTION WERE DEAD WRONG!*

But no! I followed a man and refused to believe I had the right to do what was BEST for me. In order to justify what I believed the church taught, I misinterpreted the Word, the books I read and the music I listened to. Now,

I had to undo all the damage those years had done to me AND FORGIVE them, but most of all MYSELF FOR ALLOWING IT TO HAPPEN!

It is the reason today; I do not study the Word of God like I once did—I AM *TRYING TO UNDO THE DAMAGE.* I no longer just read Christian books but all kinds of book for knowledge and understanding because I AM TRYING TO UNDO THE DAMAGE. *AS A MATTER OF FACT, I very seldom read Christian books at all because many of them still endorse the submission of women to their husbands. I AM TRYING TO UNDO THE DAMAGE. I do not just listen to gospel music, but I listen to a variety of music for inspiration and encouragement, because—*I AM TRYING DESPERATELY TO UNDO THE DAMAGE. *(Most of the time, I can hardly understand what is being said in gospel songs anyway, because the music is much too loud.)*]

Believe me when I say, I stuck an imaginary pin in that phrase from that day to this one. *"FREE A LONG TIME AGO",* will always remind me that God is my father, my guide, my friend, my counselor and my hope—not Man. I will always respect my leadership but BY THE GRACE OF GOD, AND HIS MERCY, I will never again, put ALL MY HOPE AND CONFIDENCE IN A MAN. Psalms 118:9]

CAREFUL PLANNING

When I returned home I began my preparation to leave. I started pulling together what I needed to take with me—primarily clothes for me and my children—I did not have time to take anything else. I noticed my neighbors across the street from us were at home. It was unusual to see their cars parked in front of their house so early in the day. I told my children's father I had to visit a neighbor and I would be right back. I didn't wait for an answer—I just quickly ran across the street.

I asked my neighbor if I could use his telephone. *Legal Aide had given me the telephone numbers and addresses of two or three homeless shelters in the city which catered to women like me, running from an abusive spouse.* I couldn't give them a number where they could reach me, but told them I would call them back. I called one shelter on Chicago's far southwest side, and the woman on the other end listened patiently as I explained how I needed a place to stay with my two children.

She asked me when I would be coming. I told her I planned to arrive the next day after I picked my children up from school. The woman gave me the address—and I told her I would see her soon. She and her husband ran this shelter; and although she was uncertain that he would welcome new occupants at this time, I was told to come anyway and she would speak to him.

I would later learn that this particular shelter was one of the best Chicago had to offer. At the time I called, this husband/wife team was clearing out certain occupants because of rule violations. The breaking of certain rules placed the residents in harms way because they never knew if one of the women would open the door to one of their assailants—primarily, THE ONE THEY WERE RUNNING FROM. If they did not get rid of the violators, all residents would be in danger of being hurt because of the indiscretion of one or two others.

PRECIOUS MEMORIES, HOW THEY LINGER

I felt obligated to explain to my neighbors what I was planning to do. I felt an explanation was in order not just because they were helping me, but because a friendship had really developed between them and me over the years. *Their demonstration of love for one another and for family, was remarkable—something I had never experienced.*

As I left their house, I knew what I had to do and prepared myself to leave the disaster that had lasted much too long. As I entered my own home, I reflected on this 30-year-old brick bungalow I had tried to call home. It was the first home we bought together. My son was only a toddler at that time, but there was such a nice back yard for him to play in and the detached garage gave the yard a closed-in look, for his safety. We had two bedrooms, an enclosed porch, kitchen, dining area, an unfinished basement, and an attic. I loved it so much because the potential for expansion was great. I loved living in a residential neighborhood with only a few apartment buildings scattered here and there. It was a great place to live with great families on both sides of us.

Our front yard was manicured like our neighbors—reflecting the pride we all had. In fact, my children's father saw to it that the outside of our little abode was always looking good. However, the inside of our home was a horse of a different color. *He refused to paint and refurbish the inside of our home because he said I was not worth it. The house was never clean enough and the food I cooked was not good enough. Nothing I did pleased him.* In the meantime, he was always painting someone else's house; fixing someone else's furnace, plumbing and/or wiring in their homes. He did good work and someone was always asking him to come over and help repair this or that. It was the way he got to know so many people in our neighborhood, by being so available and so helpful. Moreover, he was known and appreciated by many in the community.

I looked at my new sheer white drapes in my dining room window. They were so pretty. It took me weeks of saving in installments to finally purchase them—they certainly did something for the room. But this along with every piece of furniture and bedding I had would be left behind.

SOME THINGS I WISH I COULD FORGET

It is funny to me how I remember some things like it just happened yesterday—although I wish to God, I could create a memory loss on demand. For instance, I wish I could forget the Sunday I came home early from the 11:00 service and found a naked woman with my husband in my bedroom. To make a long story short, my children's father kept pleading for forgiveness—telling me how sorry he was and with some reluctance I forgave him. A couple of days later, he reminded me of what I had seen and promised me it would happen again and again, until I left HIS house. *He said he was determined to get me out of HIS house one way or another.*

I wish I could forget the day one of the young women from our church died. During that day, I was cleaning the house when I heard a break in the regular television programming. I stopped working long enough to hear the news bulletin. The voice said a woman had been thrown to her death over her apartment railing to the ground below by her husband. I saw her picture and I realized I knew the woman because she and her mother were members of my church.

I was so shocked that I started crying uncontrollable tears. My children's father came in at that moment asking what had happened. I pointed to the television and explained that a woman we both knew at church had been killed by her husband. He looked at me and shouted that it should have been me. He repeated it and told me if I did not stop all that crying he was going to kill me, too. Do you know what happened? Out of fear of ME dying by HIS hand, all my tears dried right up. I got up and started back to cleaning the house. Do you NOW understand why I had to leave him? It was time to get out of the insanity!

RUNNING FOR SHELTER

First, I had to get our clothes into the trunk of the car, without his knowledge. He must not even suspect me of attempting such a thing. *He had told me enough times that he would kill me if I tried to run off again. But, within the last couple of months he swore HE WOULD MAKE ME LEAVE—come hell or high water.* NOW YOU TELL ME—HOW AMBIGUOUS CAN YOU GET? With the last threat, he GUARANTEED that I would be the one to leave—but HIS children would always remain with him; he would see to that (and they eventually did).

So, that morning I took the children to school as usual, but this time I spoke to one of the teachers. *I do not remember her name, but she had been truly instrumental in maintaining some type of sanity in my life that week. It was her shoulder I cried on when night after night my children's father played his music so loud, my children nor I could not sleep.* My children and I were all rest broken and out of sorts each morning.

They had been crying the last couple of mornings I dropped them off. I would beg this same teacher to watch out for my kids because they were moody and we were having problems at home; and, frankly, I was not sure what I was going to do. She told me she would pray for us and the situation. On that day I was glad to inform her I was finally leaving the children's father. I have had enough and I was not ever coming back. So, that morning I thanked her for her kindness and her compassion towards my family. She was happy for me and wished us well. She also suggested that I inform my other child's teacher that we were moving out of the area. She would wait to hear from us—to know what school they were attending—then she would send their school records there. Leaving my children in school, I returned to finish what I had started.

When my children's father was at home, I was doing house work; when he left, I would place our clothes in the trunk of the car. When he returned home, I was cleaning the house. When he walked down the street, I was placing our clothes in the trunk. This went on all day. When the end of the school day came, I was ready to pick up the children from school, as usual. And as usual, their father screamed (for the last time), "Make sure you bring my goddamn car back here!" He never knew I would not be returning. I picked up the kids and went directly to the shelter.

We were welcomed warmly but I was apprehensive about keeping the car with me, for two reasons. First, the car was not in the best running condition. If it broke down, no mechanic on earth could fix it, because the children's father rewired it that way. Second, I did not want him to locate me—finding the car meant finding me and my kids. So I actually left the kids at the shelter, drove the car back to the house and returned to the shelter on the bus. I could not believe I was free at last.

STEPPING OUT ON FAITH....

Many things happened after I left. I lived in the shelter for six months, not telling anyone but my pastor and his wife where I was. I did not want family members to know where I was living because I was afraid someone (I did not know who) would tell the children's father where I could be found. What resulted were some hard feelings between my family and me because of that decision. Even after I told them where I was, they never visited me. They were acutely offended because I had the audacity to make a decision without their knowledge and without their input.

My son left me about a week later after I entered the shelter. He was about 13 years of age at the time and I guess he missed his dad. However, one day, he raised his hand to hit me when I said something that made him angry. I informed him on that day I KNEW HE HADN'T LOST HIS MIND. *I knew he saw his father hitting me* and I knew HE SHOULD HAVE KNOWN BETTER. I let him know—if he had ANY THOUGHTS THAT MADE HIM BELIEVE, HE WAS GOING TO TREAT ME THE SAME WAY HIS FATHER HAD—he had BETTER THINK AGAIN!!!!

Since the shelter forbade any kind of corporal punishment, he and I had some *very deep discussions and I told him repeatedly that if he could not get himself or that attitude of his together, I would send him back to his father. One day he told me I did not have to send him back,* "I know my way back home!" *I also informed him that that door would swing only one way, and that is "out" if he ever left me.* He packed his clothes and left THAT day—leaving me standing at the front door of the shelter, crying like a baby. *He NEVER knew just how bad he had hurt me.*

But, those tears did stop falling! When he found his way back home, he lied through his teeth, saying I had thrown him out. This led family members to whisper among themselves.

Finally someone asked me how I could have thrown my own son out. I could hardly believe my ears. I then told them exactly what happened. Now, I could hardly wait to see him: and when I did see my son, I set the record straight. I told him, he'd better not ever lie on me like that again—as long as he lived.

Oh, yes, I was still going to church—mostly on Sunday mornings—because there was an evening curfew I had to adhere to. There were no exceptions to that rule. Moreover, the church was still my life and I gradually began to attend church services as regularly as I had before I moved. Eventually, when I felt comfortable giving people our address, some of the saints would drop my daughter and me off at the shelter, after the church service had ended. (For that, I was truly grateful, because up until then I would be on the bus coming back.) I made it a point not to tell anyone what was happening in my life, especially about the pending divorce; but when my children's father returned to the church, everyone knew our business.

I HATE THE DEVIL WITH A PERFECT HATRED...

During this time of transition, I kept praying two prayers. My first prayer was a hope that

I WOULD NEVER HAVE to return to THAT marriage—I did not WANT ANOTHER repeat. Although, I had left with my pastor's blessing, I still had a nagging suspicion that for some reason I would HAVE TO GO BACK. When my children's father realized I was not coming back, he renewed his membership to the church, looking pitiful and lying from the pillar to the door post; pleading his cause with the people who would listen, before, during, and after church service.

When my pastor heard about my husband's return, he told me, if he could, he would personally turn him out of the church—something he's seldom done during his pastorate. He said he could count on one hand the number of people he actually turned out of the church. Because of his health, he was seldom at church anymore and he had left the church in the hand of an assistant pastor—who could not perform such an important function in the ministry. So, I was pretty much on my own to handle the return of my children's father.

Meanwhile, the father of my children was singing the blues and looking remorseful. The scenario was beginning to look like I was the culprit—it was me tearing my family apart. Some of the people in the congregation started to believe him and gave him a listening ear or would try and question me. Their talking to me was of no affect; I was not fooled and wondered how people in the church could be so gullible. Whenever he tried to pull me aside to plead his case, I would just simply walk away—I did not need to give him an explanation. If and when I saw him, I made it a point to stay out of his path.

As the drama dragged out a couple of the brothers in the church would eventually block his advances and help me to escape his harassment. One would take him aside and talk with him. The other one told him to get lost and leave me alone. I was thankful for those moments because at times it could become unbearable. There was no decent communication between my children's father and me because there wasn't any inclination left in me to correspond in any way with him. The truth was I was deathly afraid of him; I knew all that pleading and charm he radiated was not genuine. It was just a cover up that I knew all too well.   And I still had a nagging feeling I might have to return to that house with him.

I was beginning to have nightmares of my returning home, nearly every night. I would wake up in cold sweats, sometimes even screaming because I saw myself back in that house while he was screaming epitaphs like, "So you thought you got away! What on earth made you feel like you could escape me?"

My second prayer correlated with the first prayer. "Hear, O Lord, when I cry with my voice, have mercy also upon me and answer me…leave me not, neither forsake me, O God of my salvation." This line is taken from the 27th Psalms.

Certainly, the Word of God had always been an anchor for me. I may have interpreted it wrong many times, but right or wrong—the Lord knew my heart. I was finding *renewed hope,* in His Word. The reassurance never ended and asking for Jesus to help me to move courageously forward in the midst of my situation—was all a part of that prayer. And you know what? The Lord never left me alone and I NEVER WENT back either.

I KNEW THE LORD WOULD MAKE A WAY....

When I left the shelter, I moved into the apartment my pastor and his wife had occupied over the church. They had purchased a house and were gracious enough to offer me their place. I learned to love it there with my daughter and it was my very own apartment. I only had to go downstairs to attend church services and the school nearby was superb. I had lived there for about six months when someone started a fire downstairs.

An Arab American had opened a store in the front of the building and I lived over that store. Word spread that a competing Arab in the neighborhood had started the fire. But, I somehow suspected my children's father had set it, although I had no proof. He realized I was not coming back. He had threatened my life so many times I naturally felt he was quite capable of starting a fire, since he knew where I was living. My daughter later confirmed it, saying she actually saw him hanging around the building the night before.

My mother and father offered me their basement apartment, and I took it reluctantly. Moving back with my mom and dad, I felt as if I was taking a step backward. It left me wondering whether I would ever be independent again. I loved the taste of independence, but what other choice did I now have? When I moved back, I also got a part-time job because a full-time position was not available. The hours were terrible and finding someone to watch my daughter especially during the day grew into a serious problem. I was told she would not mind anyone in my family. My mother was always complaining about her attitude, and she was having problems in school. I was always apologizing to someone in an effort to try and make things right for us.

TRYING TO HOLD IT ALL TOGETHER

My daughter was around 11 or 12, and it was a terrible time for a child, who was constantly moving with her mom. I finally gave up my job so I could be with my daughter during the evenings. I also decided to go back to school to acquire some employability skills. I attended a junior college nearby and pursued a certificate in secretarial science with hopes of securing a decent job. Although my progress in school was great, my daughter and I were having problems. [Years later, my daughter shared with me exactly what was going on with her at that time—it was so unbelievable, I told her SHE NEEDED to write a book.]

My daughter told me she wanted to go back home to her father. Every time she would visit him (and her brother) she would come back angrier at me than before. *I would learn later that her father was purposely manipulating her, telling her how much she was missed and that I had broken the family up. If she would come home, I would come back too.* So she was hoping I would. She was at that age where everything was changing and we both were having a terrible time coping.

We were arguing all the time. She was discovering boys and (I had to admit,) she had more telephone calls coming in, than I did. I was also working with a social worker at the time. This is when I discovered my child had an audio/visual problem, which meant she did not always understand what I was saying but often acted as if she heard me. I had to learn how to handle her differently. Now, for me this was a blessing because I had done all I knew to do.

Chastising my daughter would have to change. I was whipping my child with an extension cord, when I used corporal punishment. My wrists were weak and I was unable to use a belt. I had been whipped with a cord when I was young— and although I did not like it and I never wanted to use one on my own children—I eventually did. But get this. While in the marital home, I was the one who whipped my kids. The children's father seldom if ever whipped them. I guess he was looking a little better to my children, than me because I was always the one who issued the punishments.

[When I think about it now, I realize I whipped them BUT he whipped me. He was the good guy, he never hit them—but he took care of their villainous mother when she needed it. *Maybe that is why they thought their dad was so great; he had become their deliverer. Mom WAS WRONG HITTING THEM and their DAD WAS RIGHT, HITTING HER—FOR THEM! There has to be a truth in there somewhere although I cannot verbalize it right now. But to me it APPEARS TO BE QUITE DEEP!]*

When my son turned about 11 or 12, his father told me to never hit the boy again, that HE WOULD CHASTIZE HIM. My children's father had told me to take care of the girl because she was the "fast one." He said she was a liar and that she was the one we needed to watch. I did not totally agree, but I did not want my daughter to be "wild" either.

What I did notice is that she did appear to be quite angry or disagreeable, and I did not want her to get out of hand. What I did not know at that time and not for some years to come is that my daughter caught her dad doing some things he should not have done. She would tell him he was wrong and she became his conscience. He did not like it, especially when his son would not speak of these things. She was the only one who would remind him. Unknown to me, this was the real reason he wanted me to correct her—and this is what I tried to do.

INTERVENTION IN HER BEHALF

When the social worker discovered my method of hitting my daughter with the cord, she told me to stop. *She explained that my daughter could be talked to and that I needed to understand that my daughter did not understand what I wanted her to do. I needed to make sure she understood what I was telling her, before punishing her.* Moreover, when I did punish her, make sure it was not with an extension cord. I did stop and today I still appreciate her intervention in behalf of my daughter.

I followed up by enrolling her in an after-school program. I felt it was going to help both of us. However, when my daughter continued to say she wanted to live with her father, I was becoming gravely concerned. One day, the arguments between my daughter and I became so bad over her desire to leave, I told her (like I did her brother), if you leave, the door only swings one way. "If you leave me, there is no guarantee you can come back." She, just like her brother, said she wanted to leave and did not want to stay with me anymore. I showed her the door, some car fare and she left. Her father came back later and goes into my apartment to get her clothes. I could not believe my daughter had actually left me, to live with him.

In the meantime, my children's father had married my pastor's youngest daughter who was also my daughter's godmother and they had a baby on the way. *I did not want my daughter in that environment—I wanted her and needed her here with me—I was the mother—no one could love her like I could.* When I met with a group of social workers who had come together to discuss my case, they all suggested my daughter would do better if she was with her father and let her stay there. My keeping her was not in the best interest for my child. If we were not careful the child could manipulate us and move back with me when she was angry with her dad; and move back with her dad when she was mad at me. As long as I did not have to give up total custody, I felt that this was only a temporary setback.

I DID NOT UNDERSTAND

(No one knew I had prayed a prayer before the Lord in regards to my daughter. It was after my son had left me. When I would attend

Sunday morning services and see my son at church with his father and his wife and not with me—that hurt me very deeply. I knew I could not deal with this situation if my daughter moved back with them too. I felt like my heart couldn't take it. So I told God I would be ready to leave Chicago, should that occur. Leaving the church I grew up in to attend another one in the city would not help me—would not give me the relief I needed. The only way I could go on would be to leave the city—I would no longer have a desire to live there any more. I asked the Lord if my daughter ended up leaving me permanently, to please let me know when it would be time to go.)

For my daughter's part, she thought she had the best of all worlds, to live with her father and her brother and her godmother. I reluctantly let my daughter go, not knowing her father's promises to her.

I never imagined I would receive the news so soon. I was in school and working near the computer's mainframe when I received the call. When I answered the phone, the social worker told me—I had to give my children's father full custody of my daughter. They all agreed that the father's environment was more stable. My daughter was familiar with the house, the neighborhood and the neighbors. She would be with her paternal father, her godmother, her brother, a new sibling on the way and the friends she grew up with. I, on the other hand, had moved too much (I offered her no stable dwelling or school to attend). I was now in school myself and living on welfare. I asked her what about me and my feelings. She said she was not concerned about my feelings; she only cared about the welfare of my daughter.

She was gone, just like that. I did not know I was feeling faint, all I knew was that I was feeling sick. I staggered out of that room and fell into the arms of one of my professors who was coming up the hallway. He just let me cry in his arms, while I sobbed long and hard. "I have to give my daughter up. They are taking my daughter away from me." He held me tightly and let me cry. When I found the strength to stand up on my feet, he asked me if I was all right. He told me how sorry he was. I don't remember whether I sat down or walked away.

However, I do remember the day I went downtown to sign the papers giving my children's father full custody of my little girl. Perhaps a day later, I was in school working on an assignment at a computer and I remember feeling like I needed a good drink to ease the pain. It got so bad I could visualize myself sitting on the floor in the corner of a room with my legs spread apart; crying as if for a long time, with a large bottle of Jack Daniel's or something comparable to it, on the floor before me. I could see myself inebriated and I could see I did not care anymore.

But, the Lord, who is rich in mercy, kindness and understanding, saw me even then. While sitting at that computer, I began typing. At first, I thought it was just words. As the tears began to fall down my face, I thought it was a poem. No; it was a song on my heart and this is what I typed:

Is this all that life can offer, is this all.

Is this all that we can hope for, is this all.

God gave us the answer, a long time ago

And I know this isn't all, this isn't all.

Now that the spirit of God, Is within me,

I'm not a servant of sin no more

I don't depend on temporal things,

My hope's, in serving the Lord.

This is why I fast and pray,

For I see a better day
And I know this isn't all
This isn't all.

It still amazes me how God comforts me just when I need it most. How could I have known that the Lord would use a song to lift my heart even while I was going through this personal loss of my daughter? Then I, can in turn, bless the hearts of others.

Shortly after that, I was asked to sing a song at a funeral. The granddaughter of one of the women at our church had died. The young woman had been living in California when someone came to her door and shot her in the face, point blank. I remembered how pretty she was, but I did not know her as well as I knew her grandmother. She and I were around the same age and I thought it a privilege to sing at her funeral. I used the song I wrote, to minister to her family on that day and her family seemed to appreciate what I had done. Before the funeral, I added the next verse.

Now when life as we know it is over
And we see our blessed Lord

He will wipe all our tears away

We won't know sorrow, anymore

Eyes nor ears have heard nor seen

What God's prepared for me

And I know this isn't all

It isn't all.

God continues to have a way of making a difference in all of our lives.

The consultation, the hearing and the release of custody followed. That was in 1986. I also heard a small, still voice in 1987 tell me, "It's time to go." I had been preparing to leave Chicago, for about a year, but I didn't know when. A year earlier, I had gone to Detroit, where my Uncle lived. He had an unoccupied second floor apartment in his one-family flat.

I had discussed with him the possibility of letting me have the apartment, if and when I decided to leave Chicago. He had said it would be there whenever I decided to come. In the early summer of 1987, I returned to Detroit to check the status of my application to Wayne State University (WSU)—I had been accepted!

WHEN I REMEMBER....

I received my associate's degree in liberal arts in May of '87, and was prepared to pursue my degree in Business Education. (It was a dream I had right before I married. It was almost lost—but here I was ready to pursue a long lost desire—leaving me feeling—for the first time—full of hope.) I also received the Wall Street Journal Award for Excellence and was asked to write an acceptance speech for that award. When I remembered all that I had gone through, the hurts; the feelings of not being quite good enough; the rejections; and the disappointments to get to that point in my life, my tears began to fall when I stood before the faculty and the other students. I told them about my struggle to do something special with my life.

I couldn't stop crying as I explained how ever step I took became stepping stones to get me where I had arrived. Had it not been for school keeping me focused, I do not think I could have made it. I started school to obtain a certificate in secretarial science—to better my condition—to strengthen my job skills in order to secure decent employment. I saw instead an opportunity to get a degree that would propel me to pursue my long forgotten dream of becoming an educator.

I was realizing my love for education, my love for learning and a desire to share that with the students I would one day touch. As a non-traditional student I appreciated every experience that came my way in that college because I always knew there was a better way of living. Every club I joined reminded me of that. Every conference I attended opened my eyes to things I have never seen or heard before. I had chosen a different world, a better world; and I now embracing a precious opportunity I had only dreamed about.

I told them I would be attending Wayne State University (WSU) (even before I knew I had been accepted) and I would be a blessing to the children who awaited my coming. I shared how happy I was to receive such an award and I promised I would never make them ashamed. Every one present, faculty and students alike cried with me on that day because I spoke from the depths of my heart. They congratulated me for my efforts, my success and for a job well done!

In the meantime, I had contacted my uncle and told him when to expect me because I was now ready to leave Chicago. The hardest thing I had yet to do at that time was to tell my children, I was going away. I did not want them to think I did not love them; I did not want them to think I was abandoning them. (Actually, they were the ones who had abandoned me.) I wanted them to understand it was something I had to do, and to do it I had to leave them for a while. *[I actually believed I would come back to Chicago once I had received my degree, never knowing I would not return. Falling in love with Detroit was not on my-things-to-do list.]* But leave them I must. Most of all, I was not happy living there anymore and grew weary with each passing day. I knew I had to be diligent, but I was determined to make this move. I knew failure was not an option. So, with extraordinary courage and a new-found strength I began....

. . .

Part Two

TRUSTING MYSELF

My Travail!

(My Discovery and Recovery of Self)

CHAPTER 8

One day at a time, that was what I had to learn—to take one day at a time. After about a year of living in Detroit and working at WSU, one of the supervisors at the Office of Minority Recruitment took me aside. He had to tell me how I had blossomed—I was looking so much better than I was looking, the first day I arrived there. He said, "You were looking like a kitten that had been beaten up. You scared me, but I was afraid to ask you what had happened to you, that you looked so bad. I could only pray for you and hope that what ever you had been through would soon end." He wanted me to know, I had come through! I had passed with flying colors. I had turned into a beautiful woman. I had to give him a great big long hug for that compliment.

— My Personal Reflection

When I told my children I was leaving, they looked like they understood, but I don't really think they could fully comprehend the scope of my departure. I had spent the day with them and tried to explain it. Then I had to let them go so I could go forward with my life. Had I known that I would be alone the day I left, I might have requested that my two children be there with me. Who knows; maybe someone would have brought them.

Moreover, the day I left Chicago, I was all alone. There was no one to see me off at the bus terminal, no tears, but my own, and no one to hug, except my brother-in-law who wanted my bus pass (since the month was not entirely up yet) to give to my niece. It really was good that it was raining hard that day—no one could tell whether my face was drenched with rain or with the tears that rolled down my cheeks. I was afraid of what was before me, but I couldn't go back to what I had left!

After arriving in Detroit, enrolling in the university and securing a clerical position in WSU's Office of Minority Recruitment; I discovered that a walk from the bus stop near West Grand Boulevard and Third Avenue to the school was just what I needed.   That street had very little traffic on it at that time of the day; and I would utilize that solitary moment to cry all the way to work. I couldn't help it. I couldn't understand why my children were not with me. I had given them life, raised, and loved them with all of my heart; but I couldn't understand for the life of me why I was in this brand new city, all alone.

Then I would wipe the tears away, go to the restroom when I entered the building, wash my face and go to work.   This went on for about a couple of weeks, I'm sure. But one day, as I did my daily walk the voice of the Lord spoke to me and said "I did it for you." I understood immediately that the events surrounding my children were done to help me to go on with my life. I was able to concentrate on school and complete my goal of becoming an educator. Perhaps if my children were with me, I could not have done it. I tell you, God has a way of working things out just for me. It was all I needed to know. God dried my eyes that day and that burden I carried was lifted. When I wiped my face that day, I never cried like that again.

TALKING ABOUT A REALITY CHECK!

After moving to Detroit, I learned two things. *Don't ask anyone for any money and do not depend on anyone except myself. I must say, those were two of the hardest, but two of the best pieces of advice I have ever had to practice...* and I did that. My uncle was the sharpest man I have ever known. I lived with him for about eight years. We had many conversations which are priceless to me today.

We often talked about: relationships; politics; our health; his young days; my young days; religion; the church; education; sex; work;

the news (current and past); our fears; our accomplishments—you name it, we talked about it. He was not perfect but he lived it and loved life to the fullest. He often reminded me that life was what you make out of it; to live it well made it beautiful. He also taught me I could make it if I took little Willie with me. Little Willie was the will to do whatever I had to do. With him on my side, I would get that degree I was after. Our uncle/niece relationship was in deed a special one. It was amazing to learn how much he was afraid of me, when I first arrived!

WHY??????

Before I got there, my mother and/or my sister informed him I was losing my mind. He was warned to watch me carefully. Neither of them ever accepted the fact that I chose to leave Chicago on my own volition. They believed my pastor's wife had persuaded me to leave. I guess they did not believe I had the good sense to do it on my own.

They believed my pastor's wife now had the power over me, they once had. It was she who told me to leave my husband. It was she who told me not to tell them where I was after I left him. It was she who advised me on everything I did. [If I led them to think that way,

I do apologize. But, yes, I made ALL THOSE DECISIONS ON MY OWN.] However, as my Uncle and I talked day after day, we became accustomed to one another and developed a good friendship. I discovered through his help that I did not have a problem—but the people in Chicago did.

For instance, shortly after I moved to Detroit, my mother would call and tell me everything that was happening in my children's home. (It had to be their father who was informing her.) When she would finish talking I would get so sick, I had to lie down. When my Uncle found this out, he called my sister and told her to tell my mother to stop calling me and telling me everything that was happening in that man's house. She stopped calling me immediately.

ANXIETY SETS IN

I cherished the long-distance calls I made to my children, because I missed them so much. I could not call everyday, but when I did they were precious moments for me. But even those moments were short-lived. When the children's father knew I was talking to them (and some times he would be the one to call them to the phone), he would simply pull the wires apart and disconnect us.   This is one tactic he used every time I talked to them.

I would get very upset, even though I soon realized that this was one of his ways to get back at me. Redialing never helped, for he'd only hang up on me again. I was not there for him to annoy me but annoy me he would, one way or another. I had to learn how to handle my anger and calm myself down. That anger would only create more frustration for me.

Visiting Chicago was not an easy thing to do either. That's when I learned about panic and/or anxiety attacks. Whenever I would return from a trip to Chicago, I would get sick. When I would lie down for the evening and I would feel as if I was smothering. Then I found myself unable to breathe. I had to quickly get up and run to the window for air. Sometimes I'd run downstairs and open the front door, no matter what the weather was like, in order to catch my breath. I even went to the emergency room at a nearby hospital. They could actually see my windpipe closing up and would give me a shot to open it back up. This went on for some time.

A sister, who was a registered nurse in my church, heard about the episodes I was having, and patiently explained to me what was happening. Up until that time, I would share my frustrations with my Uncle, but he said there was nothing he could do for this dilemma. I clearly had no idea what was happening to me. She told me something or someone was triggering the panic/anxiety attacks. Often it is unconscious and I had to consciously identify what was triggering them. I finally realized I missed my children sorely and just seeing them was hurting me so much.

When I acknowledged my missing them, *(again with many tears) confessing my frustrations, disappointments and my sadness;* I would ask the Lord to help me deal with this loss. The attacks did not stop all at once, but they no loner terrified me. Not long after that, I could lie down and go right to sleep. One day my Uncle asked me did I finally figure out what was happening to me? I told him yes and once again, we began sharing our thoughts. He told me he knew what was wrong but he wouldn't tell me because I had to figure it out for myself.

My Uncle was: my protector, a teacher of life, a philosopher, my confidant, and a source of inspiration (both naturally and spiritually). Actually we were an inspiration to one another. When his emphysema grew increasingly worse, the medication he required damaged our relationship severely and changed it for the worse. His thoughts were no longer under his control, severing the bind that held us together. Although our conversations were far and in between, I realized our love and concern for one another still remained intact. He passed away in 1997. My love for him, my respect for him and my precious memories of him left an indelible impression in my heart. He was a redeeming and consoling presence in my life and I will always thank God for having known this uniquely personable member of my family.

AS I LOOK BACK OVER MY LIFE

After I graduated from Wayne State University (WSU) in 1991, with a degree in business education, I received a master's degree in educational leadership from Eastern Michigan University (EMU) in 1998. *As of today, I have been working in Detroit Public Schools for 18 years, 15 of them as a teacher. Detroit has been good to me.* In spite of everything, I have been blessed beyond words. Yes, verbal abuse has been a part of my life as far back as I can remember. Everyone in my family has in some way or another been affected by it, even if they never admit it. And yet, I am grateful to be able to look back over my life and cherish the good as well as the bad.

After leaving Chicago, 22 years ago, and having left that marriage 25 years ago, I still struggle with self-worth. As a survivor of domestic violence, I have discovered I now have two problems: 1) To remain vigilant in stopping any kind of verbal abuse that may be directed towards me; and 2) I must STOP THE SELF-INFLICTED MENTAL ABUSE which continues inside my head.

When I left my marriage, that stopped the verbal abuse that came from him. But there remain so many other people (relatives and non relatives) who are verbally abusive as well. When I am entreated like a child by another adult, I now recognize I have to speak up for myself. I have to stop it in my own behalf—for my personal safety and for my peace of mind.

But, after all the names I've been called, and all the nasty innuendos I have endured, none of those scenarios compare to what I continue to call myself. Unconscious and conscious thoughts of my NOT QUITE BEING GOOD ENOUGH, of my NOT QUITE BEING WORTHY keeps me in the struggle to identify who I am, deep down in my heart. It is a fight because FEAR has always been my traveling companion. It usually accompanies moments when I feel my life is empty and my contributions to it have not made any difference. *When I am feeling great and think I have overcome some struggle, it rears its ugly head and the fight is on for my self worth. Identifying that fear in all of its variations has helped me to move forward because I understand its purpose.*

My joy comes in sharing what I have learned over the years. So, I have questioned the Lord about my own ministry many times. When the answer came back to me, it almost knocked me off my feet. It has taken me some time, but I am learning that my ministry is exhorting me to strengthen myself, or as the scripture declares....

. . .

Physician Heal Thyself
(The Lord Is With Thee!)

CHAPTER 9

It can be done. It is about reading all you can on loving, trusting, and believing in yourself. It about attending any thing and everything you can, that makes loving you easier. Sharing your thoughts—and affirming others in their transition. It means forgiving yourself. It means taking chances. It means moving in a direction that will cause healing in your mind, soul and spirit. It is something only you can do!

– My Personal Reflection

Understanding how to HEAL MYSELF was at first a mystery to me. Besides how does one heal ones self? I was overcoming my past and I wanted nothing better than to tell everyone who would listen that they too could overcome—I simply wanted to be a source of inspiration to others. But, healing me means continually overcoming the debilitating words and the damage they have caused me each day I have lived. That continuum has proven to be a bit more difficult as time has passed. It has left me very concerned because I often find myself in environments where negative words are often rehearsed for one reason or another.

THINK IT NOT STRANGE

Family members talk harshly at their children and to one another—and often carry a chip on their shoulders that last for generations. As a high school teacher, I hear students call each other derogatory names daily and think nothing of it because it has become a way of life. Often the parents of these same children open their mouths and I quickly realize where some of these children learned their dissemination of words. In such an environment, staff are so stressed that they are frequently ill. Under these circumstances, if I do not speak up for myself—I will find myself an object of verbal attacks on a daily basis.

The use of profanity to entertain their audience has caused the music industry to grow by leaps and bounds because they feel this is what the public (young and old bloods) relate to. Judging by the annual income derived from such garbage—they are right on the money. No wonder I must intentionally re-educate myself to speak positive messages into my life. *Trusting, loving, encouraging, forgiving and validating me is the journey I have chosen to embark upon. For without these positive reinforcements, I might as well hang my future aspirations in the wind and forget about them.*

TRUSTING MYSELF

Somewhere, a long time ago, I discovered and read a beautiful little quote that said "when you can trust yourself, then you will know how to live." My ability to trust myself is helping me to discover just how to deal with this universe one day at a time. I am so thankful that I have retained that awesome thought in my mind; and every now and then it reminds me to stay focused. I have allowed too many years to pass wherein I have neglected trusting myself. My trust in others came naturally for me. It also became easy to blame them when things didn't work out. Then I took my trust in God, as all inclusive; believing He had to do all the work. Trusting in God was based on my trust in myself; to believe in a God who actually believed in me. That meant trusting me first. If I don't believe a chair can hold me up then I will become afraid to sit in it. But if I believe that chair is sturdy enough to hold my weight when I sit in it, than I will have the confidence to sit in it. My trust in my own heart, my own mind, in my own self, will automatically catapult my trust in God. *I have to trust myself to do the right thing and believe that MY decisions and MY thoughts are as they should be.* I have to believe in ME! There is no way around it.

Some of us call it confidence; self confidence; or confidence in self. Personally, I like that. They are one of the same. I have finally discovered that TRUST IN MY SELF to overcome every thing that has held me back has proven to be an adventure (though frightening at times) that I love. It is an important part of me I have disregarded for much too long.

LOVING MYSELF

I cannot tell you how many books I have read on loving ME. However, it is truly difficult if you can not even trust yourself to do it. *One idea that I have embraced is the notion that you cannot love others until you know HOW to love yourself.* For many people, especially those of us in the church, the notion, of loving one's self has not been a very important concept.

It is as if loving one's self is synonymous with loving your neighbor. Actually, *these are two different FRAMES OF THOUGHT—and one is based on the other. How can I love my neighbor, if I do not love me? I DON'T! I TRULY CAN'T! My loving you is based on my loving me first—and not the other way around.*

Many of us, me included, have tried to live as if my loving you will automatically guide or direct you to reciprocate. That is not necessarily true. For example, I have loved my children's husband while he dogged me relentlessly. I did it believing he would somehow return the kindnesses, respect and love given to him, back to me. Instead he did the opposite and I could not understand why he could not love me like I loved him. (In my opinion, most people naturally take from others what is given freely to them—because we are naturally selfish. Sometimes we give others undying devotion when they didn't ask for it and certainly didn't deserve it. Getting that kind of love back can often prove to be harder than pulling a tooth; especially when they didn't want it or need it anyway—but you were so gong ho to give it to them anyway.) Not only that, I could not even teach him how to love me if I loathed myself.

I am just so grateful I finally figured it out. Knowing and understanding THIS—has made an incredible difference in the way I treat myself and in the way I go about loving me. Knowing I have worth has made it much easier to love me.   Knowing that loving me with the same fierceness and determination I once applied to loving others has helped me understand and cherish my own uniqueness, my own humanity and my own beauty. Why would I wish to honor and respect someone else more than I honor and respect myself?

FORGIVING MYSELF

Forgiveness is such an important part of Christian living, it is virtually impossible to get around it. As much as I would like to, I can't. But forgiving others appears to me to be somewhat easier than forgiving myself. Both are a process of sorts, but I believe forgiveness of oneself is a bit trickier. I may fool you but I cannot fool myself forever because I have to live with me 24/7; and sooner or later, I cannot continue to deny who I see in the mirror.

I have had to carry a lot of hurt and a lot of regret around because I did not speak my latent convictions. I would find myself walking away hurt, disillusioned, or angry because I did not handle a situation well. In fact, the older I get the angrier I become with myself because I thought I had overcome this aspect of myself only to find it still intact. I may not like this about myself but it is what it is—it is who I am—the other part of me I must learn to embrace as well. Whether it is the perfectionist in me or no, it is still an intricate part of me.

Therefore, I have become my own "LABOR OF LOVE" on this journey to forgive myself. I have to strive to appreciate ALL OF WHO I AM until my life comes full circle. Until I can patiently embellish and celebrate my weaknesses AND my strengths, forgiving myself will continue as an ongoing process which only the Creator can help me overcome.

ENCOURAGING MYSELF

I am learning to understand life and to appreciate it even more. Encouragement comes in so many forms but I believe it is a validation of MY WORTH. Learning to encourage myself has helped me declare and maintain my own dignity. *I cannot think of a better way to live than mastering the art of encouraging ones self.* I have a right to encourage myself until I can see and feel myself taking off with wings as an eagle because God fashioned me that way. I AM NOT A MISTAKE; I AM NOT A FOOTNOTE; I AM NOT AN AFTERTHOUGHT.

Writing a book, volunteering my time, taking up a skill, losing weight, going back to school, getting that degree, going on trips, meeting new people, attending workshops, going to the movies, going to theatre productions, writing, producing and directing plays—are only a few of the things I have done, to encourage myself. I am the better for it AND I DID NOT HAVE TO

ASK ANYONE, FOR THEIR PERMISSION! It is simply A MIND SET, WHICH HAS TO BE NURTURED by me.

That is not to say others did not contribute in my encouragement. I have met many people who have encouraged me along the way. Rather it was to LIVE AND PURSUE MY DREAMS, to express myself, to simply live— family and friends have all contributed to my encouragement. Sometimes they knew and sometimes they didn't. So, I am definitely into encouragement whether it is be for myself or for others.   I think encouragement is speaking life into the lives of men and women, boys and girls. Death and life are in the power of the tongue you know. Moreover, I just love speaking life.

Because I love to read, authors from around the world have taken me to another level. Thoreau, Emerson, Covey, Kiyosaki, Trump and so many other authors have given me hope I have only dreamed of.   I adore motivational speakers like Nido Qubein, Les Brown, and Dr. Wayne Dyer.   I do not know where I would be if not for the encouragement of so many amazing people that I have never had the pleasure of meeting.

Moreover, people are a resource that is on the outside of me. They are an outside job and

I love it when they are there for me. However, a lot of my encouragement has been an inside job. The bible, when interpreted correctly has encouraged me time and time again. When no one can be there for me, the Spirit of the Lord has never failed to encourage me. That you must know is indeed an act of faith.

Then he placed within me an ability to see beyond where I was in every phase of my life—a vision within my being to move and be better. Sometimes it comes through a poem or a song placed in my heart. More recently, I have seen more books being written and plays being written by yours truly. I even see a movie or two because it is inside of me, placed there by my creator. Encouraging myself to be all that I can be and to share with others the gifts He has placed within me, gives me purpose and makes me to know I too have something that will make this world a better place. Yes, encouraging myself has undeniably made a tremendous difference in who I am and who I am becoming.

VALIDATING MYSELF

Life is so short. There never seems to be enough time to do all I want to do. However, it is imperative to CELEBRATE MY LIFE BECAUSE

YOU MAY NOT FEEL THAT I AM ALL THAT. So MY VALIDATION OF ME *IS MUCH MORE IMPORTANT THAN YOUR VALIDATION OF ME, BECAUSE YOU MAY NOT FEEL I AM WORTH IT!* That is why I MUST EXTOL ALL OF WHO I AM.

The writing of this book has been a validation of who I was, what I have *come through and who I have become at this moment in time. It has already paved the way for who I am becoming, AND-THAT-IS-AN AWESOME THING!*

Now, to my family who do not really know me—but think they do—PLEASE DO NOT TAKE THIS PERSONALLY, BUT…

. . .

It's The Principle Of The Thing

(The Epilogue)

CHAPTER 10

(Dedicated to my cousin, Ms. D. M. Drain)

Right is right and wrong is wrong. When we call an apple an orange and refuse to call it what it actually is, we continue to lie TO OURSELVES. Justifying the lie makes the WRONG appear right. My father's name calling was wrong and his behavior was never addressed NOR QUESTIONED. When I see the same attitude in a sibling, and I CAN SEE that attitude being nurtured, I cannot deny IT IS NOT HAPPENING. I refuse to minimize the CAUSE; to do that is to prolong the longevity OF this tyrannical behavior.

– My Personal Reflection

It is interesting to me, how protective my family has been about the verbal abuse we witnessed or suffered—or at least I know I suffered. My dad was always protected from any hint of embarrassment throughout his lifetime by my mother and our immediate family. Our extended family talked about it, especially when he acted out in front of them. *Our response to them or to ourselves was to say "Jesus will fix it after a while!"; "Pay him no mind!" and "Daddy is just senile, just ignore it." Or we simply said nothing. But, I know verbal abuse has nearly destroyed my family in that our tolerance for it was ABSOLUTELY WRONG.*

GETTING A GRIP

When my dad died, his legacy included his accusations of my mother sleeping with my oldest brother, my nieces, nephews, dogs, cats, and other men on a regular basis. I remember him hiding food from my older sister and her family when she was going through some difficult times with her nine babies (and abusive husband). *He would see her coming and hide the food so they could not eat. He did this so much; I began doing the same thing in my marriage whenever a guest would come over—until I caught myself.* I HAD to get a grip.

He called everyone out of their names and most of the great-grandchildren were scared to death of him. *I guess so; his children and grandchildrenweretoo!*Nevertheless,mymother often reminded me that everything was fine! She NEVER got a grip! Mom never confronted him and would forbid me to say anything to him. However, I KNOW that confronting the abuser works. I know from experience that my dad was NOT UNTOUCHABLE AND HE WAS NOT SENILE. One day I GOT A GRIP on what we had been dealing with—and I WILL NEVER forget the day I STOOD UP TO MY DAD!

MY ATTEMPT TO STOP THE MADNESS

My uncle had been telling me the only thing wrong with my father, was that some one needed to stand up to him and tell him he was wrong. I know I thought long and hard on that idea. I never knew anyone who ever stood up to him. Well, on this particular day, on my return to Chicago—I was the chosen one.

My dad was walking around that house cursing my mother out as usual, and I had heard enough. I stood up, and I told him I was sick and tired of hearing him call my mother "bitches" and "whores". I told him as far back as I could remember he was always calling her out of her name. My dad looked at me in disbelief, and told me if I didn't like what he was saying in HIS HOUSE, I could GET OUT!

I told him I would not "GET OUT" until I told him what I wanted to say. He tried walking quickly into another room. I followed him and continued talking. I was tired of hearing him speak to my mother, the way he did. I told him I did not appreciate him cursing her out and she was unhappy because he had made her life a living hell!

I told him I hated him for that. I also said if my mother (who had high blood pressure) suffered a stroke and died while living with him, he would see my face AT HER FUNERAL for the last time. After that, he would never see me again, because I would blame him for her death. *[At some point, months later, my dad did sit down with me and questioned me about my mother dying and my not seeing him again. I told him I MEANT EVERY SINGLE WORD!]*

When he suddenly stopped walking, to glare at me, *I knew I also had to tell him about the way he had always spoken to me as well. So, I began to explain how my personal relationships had suffered because he always told me* "You are no good, no damned good, or no god-damned good!" *I never had a father who could speak to me lovingly.* "I did not know what it was like to have a man speak kindly to me—and because of YOU—I did not even know how to respond to a good man!"

My dad looked at me in disbelief, turned around and went pass me again; *walking quickly into his bedroom; and slammed the door. I opened that forbidden door* and continued to express my outrage. He pulled his gun on me and told me "if you do not get the hell out of my room, I am going to blow your damn head off." *I told him to "Go right ahead, because I am not through telling you, exactly what I THINK of YOU!" When he left his bedroom, it was apparent he was in a rage.* But MY RAGE WAS PARALLELING HIS, as I followed him throughout the house. I did not stop my dialogue with him, until I was through saying all that was in my heart.

When I finally finished, I went into a bedroom where my mother was and I shut the door. *In the meantime, my mother had been trying to calm us both down to no avail. She was now on the phone talking to my oldest sister. She begged me to talk to my sister, in an effort to calm me down. But I was fine and I had calmed myself down. I had got a whole lot of stuff off my chest and I was doing just GREAT! My* mom and I just sat and talked quietly; and the house was at peace.

I THOUGHT IT WAS A SPIRITUAL THING...

Then my father came quietly to the door opened it slightly, and asked my mom if *she was really hurt by all the names he had called her.* She looked startled and said "yes". He quietly closed the door and walked away. *Then he returned a few minutes later, opening the door ever so slightly and asked her if she would forgive him.* She told him she forgave him. Then he said "I will never call you out of your name again." He quietly closed the door and walked away. She was shocked, I was shocked, and then, I was elated. My father had very little to say to me for the rest of my visit. All I could think about on my way back to Detroit was "look at what God had done!"

I did tell you I was in a sanctified church; RIGHT! Well, when I got back to Detroit; I was the first one to stand up in testimony service. God had delivered my mother from a verbally abusive situation. I told the people what had happened and how God had stepped in and touched my father's heart and mind. *I was glad to tell them that the saints of God were not "bitches and whores." We did not deserve to be treated as such, or to be referred to as such.* Talking about some church—we had some show 'nuff church that day.

It seemed like all of the people were crying or shouting or praising God with me. *Women in particular were coming and hugging me and thanking me for my testimony.* There appeared to be one brother talking after me and he sounded angry. However, I was too caught up in the Spirit to be concerned about him.

As soon as I sat down, the Spirit of God instantly spoke to me and said "IT IS NOT A SPIRTUAL THING!" *Believe me when I tell you, my tears stopped instantly. I just sat there for a moment and pondered over those words.* I knew it was the voice of the Lord but wondered why He would say that because I was giving Him all the praise, for surely He had done this wonderful thing. Again, the quiet still voice said, "IT IS NOT A SPIRITUAL THING!" *[I did not know I would rehearse those words over and over again; for days and years to come. Nor did I know at that time I would be writing a book—with that title.]*

I thought long and hard on those words and wondered how this could be. One of the mothers came to me a couple of days later with her own testimony. Her husband had been verbally abusing her as well. After hearing my testimony, she went home and stood up to him. She told him not to ever call her out of her name again. He stopped from that day forward—honoring her request. That is when I began to see verbal abuse in a different light.

Verbal abuse is not a spiritual occurrence that needs spiritual intervention. I need not

*pray for God to send down angels from on high
to deliver me from verbal abuse. I did not need
God to send lightening bolts down to the stop
the abuser from calling me out of my name.
Verbal abuse is a learned behavior, a natural
occurrence, which needs a natural response.*
**You only need to speak up for yourself, to
stop it.** *The sooner you address it, the better.
My uncle was right! I finally got it! I only WISH
MY MOM HAD!*

SOME TRADITIONS CONTINUE

Every time I would call my mother in Chicago,
I would ask her had dad kept his promise. For a
while he had. He was no longer calling her out
of her name. She told me, "he would walk up to
me as if to say something, then he would turn
around and walk away." As time progressed,
she said he would sit down with her and ask her
if she was unhappy living with him. She started
out by saying yes, she was unhappy with the
way he treated her. With each mini-conference
he had with her, she SLOWLY began recanting
her response, until she began to say she was
really happy living with him.

Each time I called, I encouraged her
to stay strong. As time passed, he began
QUESTIONING her about his calling her out

of her name. Little by little, she began telling him it really wasn't that bad. Before I knew it, she had told him "*I really do not mind you cursing me out because I really do not pay you/ or it any attention anyway!*" Unbeknown to my **mother she had single-handedly undone the respect he had given her. Now, she was back TO SQUARE ONE**. SHE had given him the permission he needed to resume his verbal attacks on her; and he *started calling her out her name* ALL OVER AGAIN!

With me, however, whenever I was present and heard him "tune up" to call her out of her name, I would check him and he would stop speaking immediately and would walk away. I eventually told him; whenever I was present, I did not want to even hear him raise his voice at my mother. *For the remaining years he was alive, he always honored me in both of these areas, lowering his voice and never again using profanity at her in my presence. THIS IS WHY* I KNOW, *my father* WAS NOT SENILE.

THE FRUIT DOES NOT FALL FAR FROM THE TREE

When my youngest brother was discharged from the military, he had been trained as a respiratory therapist and an excellent one at that.   He was now living with mom and dad. When I returned home, I found my mother was catering to him just like she had done with my dad.   He was rude to my mother, just like my dad. He did not curse her out, but the look and the words were outright rude.   Dad was always silent because I was there and I had to tell my brother to ease off my mom. *He did, but after I left I knew what was taking place and I realized he was being groomed by my father—while my mother was validating it.*

That is why I believe the spirit of my dad took up residence in my younger brother. This occupancy did not take place the day my dad died, but over a period of time, prior to his passing.   My father later moved in with my youngest brother and had stayed with him for only a short time. It was dad's decision and my mom reluctantly went along with it.

The last time I saw my father in Detroit, was in 1998, at the funeral service for my six month old granddaughter—who had perished in a terrible apartment fire—the day before Mother's Day. My dad was well, standing straight, walking tall and looking good. The next time I saw him was at my brother's house on Father's Day, about a month later and he could hardly walk. I could not believe my dad had gone down so fast. My brother tried to complain that no one cared about dad; but I stopped him there and reminded him that he was the one who took him in and he was the one who should have made the family aware of how he was doing/or of how ill he was.

I lived in Detroit—I had no way of knowing anything—unless someone informed me (I couldn't possibly get pertinent information about my father through osmosis!). I quickly suggested if dad gets worse, take him to the hospital. I was informed that my dad was in the hospital that following weekend. He was dehydrated and some other maladies were discovered. I went to see him the following weekend and he was talking. The next week, I heard he was not talking. The next time I saw him, he was in a coma. *He died in July (of that same year) and was buried in August. That was only two days before my daughter and I turned off the life support on my two-year old grandson—whose body had succumbed to the burns from that same apartment fire.*

COMPLICATIONS IN KEEPING IT REAL

The night before my dad's funeral, I felt inspired to write something about my father and his relationship with my family. I had planned to tell the truth about him. When my mother heard I was writing something about my father for his funeral, she paced the floor back and forth. She kept reminding me not to embarrass her or the family. She said it with conviction, although she said it sweetly.

You see my dad was loved in his neighborhood and a frequent customer at the corner bar. My mom wanted to keep this love and admiration for my dad in the forefront. "Do not embarrass him or this family," she kept reminding me. Called "Rev" for short (because he use to be a preacher, so I heard), my dad kept plenty of money on him—and he spent big time—setting up his friends (and their friends) with food and drinks. He had no problem spending money on them and his women.

He had worked for General Motors for years and later he would acquire a second job at Pullman. Because of this, I never knew what ADC (Aide to Dependent Children) was like, but I did know what it was like to not have some of the things I wanted. My dad could afford to do more for his family because he had the money—but he refused to spend it on us. Behind closed doors—his family suffered quietly. *In the meantime, I had changed the tone of my paper.*

When I read my poem at my father's funeral, *I am told that family members had held their breath until I was finished. I actually do remember hearing some loud sighs of relief, when I was done.* Everyone was relieved that I did not GO THERE and TELL IT LIKE IT WAS. Instead, I had brought back pleasant memories of days gone by and for the most part long forgotten. I even caused some of them to chuckle about this and that, along the way. In essence, mom had unconsciously made dad who he was in his lifetime AND after his death: *an upstanding citizen and one hell of a father. This is what my mother wanted and this is what she got—and my contribution to the funeral pleased her. Later that evening I realized she had gotten her way again at a time when I wanted SO MUCH to be honest. I was so angry with myself because I had contributed to the deceit; never acknowledging that dad had said and done some terrible things. Neither, did I want to admit the realness of the verbal abuse I had experienced all of my life.*

My older brother and I talked very deeply that night, and he shared with me his disappointment. He thought I would at least have the courage to speak the truth. He told me, "Sis, if you had just told the truth, I think I would have gotten saved right there in the funeral home. I think I would have shouted right through the doors." *My brother just wanted to keep it real for a change. You see, he had taken a whole lot verbal abuse from my father and his friends, and nobody really knew it, or possibly cared.*

SOME CHILDREN ARE FORGOTTEN IN THE WORLD OF VERBAL ABUSE

Since, my dad was the good old boy in the neighborhood, he was also taken advantaged of—plenty of times—and had it not been for my oldest brother—he might have been seriously hurt (or dead) a long time ago. *Dad was often set up (for robberies), but his oldest son was always around—protecting him. My brother knew these people hated him, but my brother never left his father's side.* Moreover, my brother was often incarcerated because he was looking out for my father (and other family members as well).

When my father got mad at his son, he insulted him before his drinking buddies—who meant him no good any way. But dad was convinced his son was stepping way out of line. One way to get back at him was to go through my mother. My father kept accusing my mother of having slept with their oldest son.

He said this because she often sided with my brother. *So, dad would swear to my mother he knew she was sleeping with him. I think he thought she would tell my brother and felt he would become angry enough to stay away from him and his corner buddies.*

I do not know if that was the case, but it certainly did take a toll on my mother, to hear him make such a terrible accusation. She would tell me over the phone, with tears in her voice, how terrible those words made her feel. But, I don't believe she ever told my brother. *She felt if my brother had heard such an accusation coming from his dad, my brother might have killed him.* I do not know whether he knew THIS because **he kept on protecting my dad**.

Instead of my father thanking his for watching out for his safety, *dad would get angrier with him.* But verbal abuse continues because the abuser is told by people like my mother—you are okay, we're not okay. When it goes on for generations, it seems it will never stop and it only gets worse.

GENERATION OF LIES ON TOP OF LIES

For years, my mother told me her father (my grandfather) was as good as one gets. She felt his legacy was always tainted with rumors

174 It Is Not A Spiritual Thing!

that were unfounded. My mother being the baby girl said her father was a really good man and father...even preached a few times in his later days. But my uncle was the one who had informed me on the REAL DEAL.

My maternal grandfather was a womanizer who was always fighting my grandmother. It started when they were newly married. At first grandma could handle herself very well and my grandfather would have a run for his money. But as she started having children (13 in all) her strength abated—but he never stopped fighting her. [Why did my grandmother have to defend herself from the get go? Why did he have to PLAY like that with the future mother of his children? Why did the white landowner tell my grandfather he really knew how to handle his wife and later tell him, he really knew how to handle his children? Why did my grandfather feel and demonstrate such PRIDE in himself after hearing such accolades? Why did my mother take great pride in my father having never hit her, but did not consider the names he called her abusive? Why did I, as a child try to please everyone with the hope I would not be told I was how stupid I was? Why did I not recognize the name calling in my marriage was only preparing me for the physical abuse

It's The Principle Of The Thing

that would follow? Why did I take it? Why did I accept the lies? Why are there women today willing to go through hell and high water to stay with men who denigrate them every single day? Why are there some men who live the same way with their women?]

There were times that the violence against my grandmother had gotten so bad that all of her children would crowd around their mother while she was sitting in a chair, and beg their father—"Oh, papa, don't kill mama!" These truths I finally learned. When I confronted my mother—she said she doesn't remember such episodes. How does one grow up in the same house and not know such things? It is possible—with generations of children—it certainly is possible. My family is a perfect example!

IT IS THE PRINCIPLE OF THE THING

Later that night after my oldest brother had left, my youngest brother came by. I had heard at the repast, my mother would not get dad's car. I wanted to know if this was true. He said, "Yes, it was dad's will that mom not get anything." I asked him about a will. "Daddy did not have a will." Whatever dad had, he himself would get it—including all monies from the bank. I did not know just how to respond, but I mumbled something about mom having rights; she had been his wife for almost 50 years. He told me "Mom had no rights based on the way she treated my dad". I got upset and just walked away. *I later pondered over what he said about our mother.* SHE HAD NO RIGHTS! SHE HAD NOTHING COMING BECAUSE OF THE WAY SHE TREATED MY DAD??????_

When I thought of all the times she tried to protect my father; justify his neglect of his family; made him look good in the eyes of his friends; cooked and prepared his meals every single day, before the sun was up to sun down; permitted him to curse her out just about every day of their marriage; justify his other women in his life; washed and ironed his clothes; hear him talk about her daughter and her children; continually picked him up from the floor when he was as drunk as a skunk; constantly mopped the urine off the floor where he left it when he passed out; then put him in the bed; get scared out of her wits when he would drive drunk and have the car spinning out of control in the dead of winter—and sometimes she had to beg him to let us out and we took a bus home—I honestly wondered, WHAT WAS HE TALKING

ABOUT????? THE WAY <u>SHE</u> TREATED MY FATHER???!!!!

She treated him like a saint. *Then I thought about how my brother had began treating my mom, when she was the one who brought him into this world; loved him like a mother does; bathed him when he couldn't bathe himself; breast fed him; fed him; clothed him; wiped his nasty butte; wiped his snotty nose; took him to the hospital when he was sick; cared for him at home when he was sick; wiped his tears; was always there when he needed him*—again, I wondered.

SHE WAS HIS MOTHER! HOW COULD HE DO WHAT HE WAS DOING TO HER? HOW COULD HE SAY, "DAD TOLD ME NOT TO GIVE HER A DIME?" My brother had reminded her, he had already spent some of the money fixing her furnace and carpeting her floor before the funeral. He said "I was not supposed to even do that!" WAS IT HIM, OR DID I JUST NEED TO GET A GRIP….

No! It was the principle of the thing.

Did I not try and sue him? I sure did. **It was the principle of the thing!** It didn't work, but Lord knows I tried to do what was right, because I was the only one who wanted to address this issue. I felt he was wrong and if mom was not going to take him to court for what she had a legal right to, then I was going to take him. *When I brought this up to my other siblings, they were perfectly satisfied, or so they said. For me, it was the* **principle of the thing**. *I told them my brother had now picked up the same spirit dad had and it needed to be addressed.* Their response was "let the dead alone, it is all over," or "don't try to bring him (my dad/or his attitude) back, just leave it alone."

It was the principle of the thing! But, we were all heirs to dad's money; my brother was not an only child. I just believe that spirits never die; they just take up residence in someone else's body. That same spirit was living in my brother and directing him—and I had a problem with it. ***And it was the principle of the thing.*** *I was his oldest daughter; and I knew I was within my right to say and do just what I was doing!*

WHAT'S LOVE GOT TO DO WITH IT?

When my brother tried to get information from mom about my court case, *she would call me (many times) and tell me to drop the case. She wasn't worried about it—why should I? I told her* **it was the principle of the thing.** *If* *she did not want to pursue it, then it was my choice to follow through.*

My mom (bless her heart) called me one day in Detroit and started telling me how *deeply in debt my brother was. She literally sang the blues in regards to her youngest son. (Me, I could care less.) She then referred to my need to love him and forgive—she told me "Forgiveness was becoming a **problem I needed** to deal with." She called me several times with the same concern and warning.*

The last time she called, she told me "God had told me to tell you, you needed to forgive and let go of the past." She was sounding teary over this, but she got the message over. *I tried to reassure her as usual that I am handling myself quite well and she need not worry about me. However, as soon as I hung up, I realized she had done it to me again. She was so concerned about me loving and forgiving my low-down brother that she used God, to defend her ungrateful son. She was wrong AND I HAD to tell her.*

I immediately called her back and told her as nicely as I could, *to "never call me again, telling me what God had said. I had a right to think whatever I wanted to about my brother. He was wrong and she was wrong for defending* him."   She got quiet but she heard me out. *I then called my oldest sister and told her what I had told mom. She thought I was wrong, but I reassured her I was not. My mother has always played these kinds of games with me—taking me a guilt trip. My mother felt if she could make me see the errors of my ways, **I would get with the REAL PROGRAM**. My sister said mother was a little senile. (Now, it was my mother who had reached senility!)*

I said "No, she wasn't! *She had always defended that nasty spirit that was in dad and now she was trying desperately to defend that same nasty imp that was now in my brother." She told me mom had never talked to her that way. I told her it was because she had acquired a certain amount of respect from mom, which I NEVER, EVER had with her. This day, was my day, to finally demand it!*

Yes, my mother was 76 or 77-years-old at the time, but she was not too old to learn something new. *I told my sister this, not because I wanted her to ease the medicine I had just given mom, but to reassure my sister that I meant every word of it. Needless to say, my mother has never gone there with me again.*

VERBAL ABUSE MAKES YOU SEE THINGS UPSIDE DOWN

I am saying all of this to say the repercussions from verbal abuse can leave *us with something to be desired. I think it chips away at our brain like the constant dripping of water on a rock in that same spot, eventually wearing it away, so we cannot think straight.* And some times we don't even know it we can't even think straight. It makes you see things upside down, because you will see the abuser as someone who needs love, understanding and reassurance. But it makes the abused look like they are wrong, when they are right. With that kind of love, understanding and reassurance is withheld from the abused. THAT IS CRAZY. Some people call it giving up the right for the wrong; I am sorry, I call it LYING.

It doesn't matter how you look at it, its still lying. I guess we lie to ourselves so much; we convince ourselves that we are telling the truth! *Calling right wrong and wrong right is not what God is calling the people of God to do in this day and time. Defending those who are wrong simply does not make sense to me anymore. I ALSO HAPPEN TO BELIEVE WE NEED ALL (and not just a portion) OF OUR FACULTIES IN*

*GOOD WORKING ORDER TO HANDLE THE
PROBLEMS THIS LIFE WILL BRING.*

*All of us wanted to be loved and my brother is
no exception. It is wrong to pit children against
children in a household but it happens and will
continue in many more households. My brother
is a great person and a great father, but he like
all of us have done something that made other
family members upset. [Today, my brother and
I still argue who the black sheep of the family is.
He seems to think HE IS THE CHOSEN ONE,
BUT I THINK I HAVE HIM OUT NUMBERED
BY AT LEAST NINE YEARS.]*

CHOOSING TO LIVE

I cannot speak for any of my family
members—but I believe each of them is
doing all *they know to live their best life in this
world. For example, each of my siblings are
entrepreneurs in their own right. My oldest
sister still amazes me and I can see how much
alike we are in so many ways. She is all that
and more. She has so many children, grands
and great grands, I believe she has her private
nation. She remains the glue that keeps them
all together. My youngest sister is an incredible
lady and tries to make a difference in the lives of
our family every chance she's given. I believe*

we are closer today than we have ever been. She is a private kind of lady but a great listener and loves God so much. I only pray that every desire in their hearts will come to pass. They all deserve it.

With my mom, I really never had a dragged out fight with her. She can be so sweet and humble at times—I could never come at her like that. But, I have had to remind her on how she wrong she was on several occasions. I can only love her and forgive what I remember she said and did. She like every loving mother that has ever lived did her best to teach us the difference between wrong and right. She is still alive today and I thank God for her—and for His teaching me how to love and appreciate her.

We are all a drum major of sorts in our own individual world. Each one has their own drum beat that he/she must follow. I forgive my dad, even though he is six feet under, and I miss him very much. *At least I told him how I felt and I saw the change in him, and that is all I could ever ask.*

God has given me life, and I h*ave spent most of that life in fear. Fear of losing friendship, fear of upsetting loved ones; fear of failure and of not quite coming up to par. When life becomes so encumbered with regrets and feelings of* *worthlessness; when one feels that life has not been a productive one; that everyone's opinion is considerably better than one's own—the meaning of life loses something. Many times, I have come to the point that I had lost an interest in living. But, the Lord in His infinite wisdom and love did not leave me that way. I choose to live because it is ordained that I LIVE AND DECLARE HIS WORKS.*

It is a wonderful thing to know I have a right to celebrate who I am. *This book has turned into a celebration of me because I realize my life does have importance and significance; and for this I am truly grateful. It is a marvelous thing to know I am a beautiful creature of value and of substance. As I contend to call those things that are not as if they were, I realize I must be steadfast in decreeing my worth. For, I am a great woman, and only my creator is greater than I.* I love the way He loves me and I love the way He's teaching me to love and trust Him. But, most of all, I will always love and cherish the way He has revealed to me the need to LOVE MYSELF. When I long so desperately to be loved by a good man, I remember I have had a man in my life lying right next to me—and realized at that moment although his warm body was lying next to mine, a terrible loneliness was gripping my heart at the same time. I understand that you can have a significant other in your life and still feel extremely lonely.   I had rather be in solitude than be with someone who really doesn't care about me. And that is why I know that loving myself is paramount today.

Then I constantly have to remind myself how extremely important it is to TRUST MYSELF!!!!! I have seen many great people enter and exit my life. Their testimonies to what God has done for them still excite me. But to trust others to lead me forever has fallen short too many times for me to count. Each of us have a calling on our lives… and to trust that God is leading me like He is leading you is to me what serving a great God is about. For there is no one quite like me and there will never be one like me again. There is no one like you and there will never be anyone quite like you again. What God has for me is for me. What God has for you is for you. I have to trust myself enough to believe God. You have to trust yourself enough to believe God too.!

How God will use me leaves me in Great Expectation because I KNOW HE LOVES ME–JUST-THAT MUCH! And no one but no one can love me that much! THAT IS BECAUSE MY

TRUST IN HIM AND MY TRUST IN MYSELF IS NON-NEGOTIABLE.

Verbal abuse is not a spiritual thing, but a precursor to the physical abuse that is to follow! Sooner or later, it needs to be recognized for what it really is!   This is my testimony.   This is my story.   But, it is merely a glimpse of the magnificent journey I am on. I hope it has been as much of a blessing to you, as it has been for me.

. . .

An Interview With
The Author

CHAPTER 11

For me this book has brought out of me some things I did not expect. I knew it would be a blessing to me, but I never imagined acquiring an understanding that would exceed my expectations. I am only flesh and blood—we all are—and life is a journey from birth until death. To live it, is what we are all striving to do. To live it well is our challenge.
– My Personal Reflection

How my book will be received by family and the reading public is not easy for me to foretell. *Sure, I would love my family to appreciate it and for the public to embrace it. Certainly, I want Ms. Oprah Winfrey to make it a welcome part of her Book Club. Clearly, I understand some will like it and some will not. But, this book is not about the people in it, but MY REACTIONS to the people in it.* It is indeed MY story!

The following interview is a simulation of what I anticipate what would be asked of me, about my book. It is another opportunity for you to get to know me a little bit better. I did not use a name for the interviewer but I hope you get the gist.

INTERVIEWER: How long did it take you to finish this book?

ME: *Let me see. I started it sometime before I moved to Detroit in 1987. I have been here for 21 one years. I may have started writing it in 1985 or 1986 or at least thinking about it. I am thinking 22 or 23 years. I wish I had dated the first lines I wrote.*

INTERVIEWER: *What made you think that your story was so important you had to write about it and what makes you think anyone would want to read it?*

ME: *In response to your first question. Every believer who has a personal relationship with the Lord feels the significance that personal relationship with Him brings. We have been exhorted to comfort one another and comforting other believers is a part of my ministry. I have found comfort in what other believers share with me, when I needed it the most. Moreover, other believers have found a way to convey their walk with God by teaching, singing or preaching about it. I chose the vehicle of writing. .*

The answer to your second question is, God blessed me and revealed to me something I did not know about verbal abuse. It was not a spiritual test of my faith. It was not even about spirituality. That is the message. Domestic violence is increasing and the people of God need to know they do not have to a part of THAT LIFESTYLE. I believe reading my book will help many.

INTERVIEWER: You did not mention too many family names in this book. Did your family disagree with your writing your autobiography?

ME: *Some agreed and some disagreed because it was about family. Those who agreed were generally not in my immediate family; cousins and such. My immediate family has some concerns because if it is in the family it should stay in the family. But I had a need to express myself. I have done an excellent job of holding stuff in, just to please people (and family members are people). I wrote it to validate myself, to affirm that what I have been through actually happened. I tried to be discrete by not mentioning names. My intent was not to embarrass family, but to share my experience with verbal abuse.*

My family members do not wish to talk about things we have been through, but I do. I have a right to get it out because this is about me—my own thoughts; my reactions; my failures; my successes; my regrets; my anger; my doubts and fears. Yes, I may express my thoughts based on what they said or done, but I am more concerned about <u>my reactions to them</u>. I want total healing and in my opinion, you can only be healed if you deal with what made you sick in the first place.

INTERVIEWER: *Some people choose not to rehash their past. They have claimed healing by not talking about it. You chose to talk about what you went through in order to obtain healing. Do you believe someone can discover healing from their past if they leave it alone and let God take care of it.*

ME: *Maybe some of us can do it. I will not deny that. All of us are different. If they can handle it better by not talking about, I have no problem with that. But all of us can not and I chose not to handle it that way. This is just my opinion.*

I am told there are five steps to grieving or being healed from grief of every kind. I have been totally stuck in "denial" (the first step) for a long *time. I did not believe I had married someone who did not even like me. I was told I had a problem and not him. I was told to forgive even when I did not know "Why." I was told to keep my mouth shut and not say anything to any one. I was told a lot of things which kept me from expressing how I felt for many years. How can I be healed if I cannot voice it, say it, or call it what it is? How is that done? I will not try to change anyone's mind. <u>But, please, do not try to change my mind EITHER</u>!*

INTERVIEWER: Does forgiving others still prove an issue for you?

ME: *Forgiveness was never really an issue for me. It was an ongoing issue for those around me. I felt comfortable in my own skin, but I was often told to FORGIVE when something happened to me. That may have confused me because it came from someone I loved or respected.   But learning to trust my own thoughts and beliefs was my only issue.*

I know God knows my heart because if He didn't, I'd certainly be in trouble in the eyes of man. I am a forgiving person, but you can not demand that I forgive, upon your command. That is not what I do. I tell people that whenever they think my forgiveness is necessary I remind them that it is my choice. Then I tell them it is really is between me and my God. Then I may challenge them to pray for me.

INTERVIEWER: In your first chapter you mentioned that you made yourself forget some of the things that were said to you or done to you. How did you make yourself forget?

ME: *You must understand that I did not think I had a choice. I had to live there with this man and handle it the best way I could. Some things hurt me so bad; I did this thing with my mind. I would see or hear the ugliness of that word or event and I would imagine it being placed in a beautifully wrapped box. The box had colorful ribbons and a beautiful bow. In a second, I would mentally fling the box as far back in the recesses of my mind as I could. I could see it being thrown way back into utter darkness and I would wait until it disappeared. In psychology it is called suppression, the conscious exclusion of painful desires or thoughts from awareness. I simply used a little creativity with ribbons and all.*

These visualizations were survival tactics I used. It helped me move on to the other things that needed my immediate attention. What I flung in the back of my mind, was simply too painful to linger on. Then I would forget it ever happened or it being said; unless someone brought it up to me again. Every time someone would bring back the event to me, I would argue that it never happened, until I was made to remember, that it did.

INTERVIEWER: Tell me about your education. Do you think your lifestyle of verbal abuse (as you call it) affected you at school?

ME: *Yes it did because I did not have the confidence to stand up or speak up for myself on several occasions. Had I spoken up for myself, my high school matriculation would not have suffered so. I would have completed a practical nursing program had I stood up to my instructor. After I finished college, I still did not believe enough in myself and I missed out on some opportunities to teach on the college level.*

INTERVIEWER: Other than honoring and respecting you, did your father do anything else that made you appreciate him.

ME: *When he paid for me to have corrective eye surgery. I believe that stands out as one of the things I will always remember. He had asked me what I wanted him to do or to give me as a wedding gift. I had heard eye surgery was a good option for me, so I chose the eye surgery. That was one of the greatest things he could have done for me.*

My dad also told me if I wanted to go to college he would pay for it. I wanted to go but by the time he told me, I think I had graduated from high school. I was scared to death and did not know what to do or how to do it. So, I did miss that opportunity.

INTERVIEWER: Are you telling women (and men) in the church to leave their spouses who verbally abuse them?

ME: *I am telling women and men THAT THEY MUST DO something if they find themselves in a verbally abusive relationship, for only they have the power to STOP IT. I am telling them my experiences and letting them know THEY DO HAVE A CHOICE. Actually, women (and men) in new relationships have a better chance to begin it correctly, if they make their feelings known at the beginning.*

If women (or men) choose to stay in a verbally abusive relationship, I tell them what the results can entail. They must stop it before it gets worse. Stop it before the physical violence starts. Many choose to stay in it and just argue back, physically fight back or whatever, but if children are involved, those children suffer from seeing and hearing such interactions between the adults.   It took me years to understand that.   It took me years to understand I did have a choice.   I hope it doesn't take women and men as long as it took me.   But I did what I had to do and I do not regret my decision.   Their situation may not be the same as mine, but they should do something.   It takes courage, but how can you live in a world like this and not be courageous.   That is something you need to think about.

INTERVIEWER: You have not remarried since your divorce in 1984.   Do you feel you have not married again because your standards are too high?   Or do you want to remarry?

ME: *I would like to remarry.   I am older now and I have a better understanding of what I am looking for in a man. Yes, I have standards because there must be boundaries set.   There must be a place where an action or a word is unacceptable—or there would be a free for all. Those standards might be considered too high for some, but that certainly beats the pants off having no standards at all.*

Because I have been married, I have greater insight into what a marriage should and should

196 It Is Not A Spiritual Thing!

not be. Marriage has to be based on mutual respect. The couple MUST BE ABLE to communicate WITH EACH OTHER; speaking and listening to one another. A sense of humor is a must—they must be able to genuinely laugh together—with one another and not just laugh at one another.

Actually, I have met several gentlemen in this 24 year span but I chose not to marry any of them. I have been wined and dined and treated kindly but they were not what I was looking for in a mate. They were also seeing other women when they met me. When those relationships ended all but two of them married someone else right away— and one of those two is now deceased.

I am glad I chose solitude because it gave me the time I needed just to get to know me. Knowledge of self is extremely important because I do not like making the same mistakes twice. Since I am a settled woman, I am not simply looking for a one-night stand, a bootie call if you will. I am looking for a man who wishes to settle down with me. Since I can take my own self out for dinner, to a movie, or on a trip; I have decided I can wait and trust God to bring that special gentleman to me.

INTERVIEWER: How is your relationship with your ex-husband at this time, 2008.

ME: *In September of 2008, I had an opportunity to express myself to him, for the first time, after all these years—1969 to 2008. Until then, our conversations remained superficial, strained and not good. We both were flown in by my son and his fiancé to witness them saying their wedding vows on the outskirts of Baltimore, Maryland. I told my ex what I thought about him and his wife; and did not bite my tongue. He had to be surprised because he said little to me for the rest of our stay. I am told by my son and my daughter, that they both noticed a significant change in their father after that visit.*

I regret having to take so long to communicate my feelings to him. He should have known the truth a long time ago. Christian teaching told me to forgive, forget, and get over it. I learned you better tell that significant other how you feel. When I held my frustrations on the inside he could not benefit from the knowledge, nor could I, keeping the hurt and the pain inside of me. Until I told him how I really felt, he really did not know me. How could he? I did not even know myself, for a very long time.

He passed away on Monday, December 29, 2008 from complications due to a heart attack and stroke. My mother told me up until his death he never cease asking her how I was doing. I am also told that he had gotten his life straight with God. Getting our life straight with the Creator is something we all must do.

INTERVIEWER: It appears you are only talking about heterosexual relationships in your book. Are you homophobic?

ME: *I do not know much about the homosexual lifestyle. I cannot write what I do not know anything about. But, I heard someone on the radio say; if you have problems with heterosexual relationships (especially when it comes to communication) you will probably take it into a homosexual relationship. I tend to agree because communication is too important to take lightly.*

INTERVIEWER: You say you have always been in the Apostolic or Pentecostal Faith. Do you find some of the same problems with verbal abuse exist in other denominations faiths like the Catholic or Baptist?

ME: *I can only address where I have come from. I am certain that evidence of verbal abuse can be found in other churches, but I can only speak about the Apostolic/Pentecostal Faith. There is an abundance of wolves coming in sheep's clothing there; and when you are hoping to find a good partner, you had better be EXTREMELY CAREFUL who you choose!*

INTERVIEWER: Well, Lady Day that ends our interview today. I wish you success on your first book; your autobiography. I will listen for the reviews and stay in touch.

ME: *Thank you my friend.*

. . .

My Personal Reflections

CHAPTER 12

Please enjoy this collection of poems I have written!

NEW BEGINNINGS, Written November 22, 1985 @ Kennedy-King College,

Chicago, IL @ 1:12 p. m.

*G*od has new beginnings,
He passes out now and then,

It's when you have a brand new start—
You find Him, a brand new friend.

You know you've honored Him always
To you He's always dear,
It is simply another opportunity
To show He's **EVER NEAR.**

New beginnings come in different forms,
Friends and family ties;
But, no matter how it comes about,
He's always standing by.

New pastor, classes, a brand new job
Just a few things you may encounter.
Some will come on you suddenly,
While others you slowly ponder.
Sometimes, you have an ultimatum
You must decide on today.
But many times you have no options,
All choices are taken away

New beginnings can come through sadness
When loved ones pass a way;
We pray they are in the arms of God
What more can we do or say.

But, I thank God for new beginnings
Although I can't always say,
That I truly feel on top of things
On any given day.

Sometimes, the days are very hard,
The **TIMES in between are rough.**
But the end result, is what I seek
His grace, IS, sufficient enough.

The greatest assurance that I
can find
To acknowledge His mercy
unending.
For He is my **all encompassing
Omega,**
**And my Alpha, MY NEW
BEGINNING!**

<u>**REVELATIONS**</u> <u>Written June 7, 1988</u>

—While attending KENNEDY-KING COLLEGE, Chicago, IL. 1:12 p.m.—

W hen you looked upon me
Just a few years ago,
You not only knew my future
But the way that I would go.
> You knew I needed understanding
> And patience for a guide,
> You knew I needed companions in Christ
> **For encouragement besides.**

You knew everything that would occur
And how, I'd take it too.
You knew at times, I'd not understand
You knew I needed you!
> So as soon as I stepped into this city
> Your work on me began,
> You did a new thing, in my mind
> **Replacing hope, where doubt had been.**

You were crushing the fear within me
A couple of decades old,
And still, you're working to free me
From its devastating hold.

In your quest, to set me free
Came an awesome revelation within;
With all my heart, I have fallen in love,
With you, all over gain.
So, I sought your face in earnest
With love petitions in my head
Surprised to find, the more I sought you
The sweeter my heart was led.

Just want to paraphrase your word
If you delight yourself in me,
All the desires in your heart
I will give them all to thee.
You tasted like honey in my mouth
I sought only for your essence.
On my knees, as I walk the streets
I looked forward to feeling your presence

The awesomeness of your beauty
Has been revealed in simple things.
Like in the plants, the sky, the trees
In the songs, the birds do sing.
When I first fell in Love with you Jesus,
My Savior and my King,
I thought this was all I had coming;

But there was coming, a greater thing.

Slowly I am discovering
A love I did not expect;
Love for me is coming forth,
A revelation, all by itself.
> I can love me, and you love me.
> On myself; **NOW I CAN LABOR?**
> I thought I was only—**TO LOVE GOD,**
> **THEN TURN** around **to LOVE MY NEIGHBOR.**

To undergo and to understand
I have the right, by God,
To care about me, and what I want,
Like Moses, I too, have a rod????
> In my hands, I have what I need
> To make my dreams come true,
> Finally, I think I've got it—
> **I can love me, and still, love you.**

> The songwriter said, "Jesus,
> You are the center of my joy,"
> There is no better way to **EXPRESS IT.**
> **You are what I've been looking for.**

Lord, I just want to thank you
This praise, I freely send—
For allowing me to fall in love,
With YOU AND MYSELF AGAIN!!!

WHEN I REMEMBER Written, August 5, 1998

I read this poem at the funeral of my father, (1919 – 1998)

I did my best to remember those things that made me feel good as the daughter of my father...

I remember the times he took our family to Riverview, a well-known amusement park, located on Chicago's Northwest Side. This park has long since been torn down, but the memories remain in my heart. Like how mom and dad barbecued ribs and chicken early in the morning, packed it all up and took us to Riverview. Dad would always stay in the picnic area with the food, which always included pop and ice cold watermelon. I would ride until I couldn't ride anymore. Then I would run back to the picnic area where my dad would open this feast that was fit for a king or queen. Lord only knows how much I did eat, how great I felt and how happy I was...**IN THOSE DAYS, WHEN I REMEMBER.**

I did my best to remember those things that my father did to make me feel good.

I remember when daddy would take us to White Castles. He would ask each of us "How many hamburgers do you want?" As long as we ate what we asked for, we could order as many as we like. "Daddy, I want 6!" or "Daddy, I can eat 12!" It didn't matter how many we wanted, it was never too many...**IN THOSE DAYS, WHEN I REMEMBER.**

I did my best to remember those things that my father did that made me feel good.

I remember when dad would bring home bushels of vegetables and fruit, especially during the autumn. He brought bushels of tomatoes, green and red; and sometimes peaches. But most of the time he brought fresh apples that made the whole house smell fresh and sweet. However, one of the things he did quite often, if my recollection serves me right, was to bring us two or three of those long, ripe, sweet watermelons. (My dad had a way of thumping watermelons. And sure enough they were always sweet and ripe.)

Well, he'd take that watermelon and divide it in quarters. I could not eat a whole quarter, but I'd take it and sit down on the floor that mom had covered with newspapers. I was small and my age escapes me. But I would take my piece and take my seat with the others and try my best to eat it all. When I was through, I always found it hard to get up off the floor. I was so full and laughed so hard, I would cry because every time I tried to get up, I would slip down or fall back on the floor. Cat, do you remember? She had the same problem…**IN THOSE DAYS WHEN I REMEMBER**.

**I did my best to remember those things that my father did that made me feel good**.

I remember not long before I married my children's father, that daddy asked me what I wanted him to do for me. I told him there was a surgical procedure I wanted to have. Doctors believed they could straighten my left eye, which turned inward, because the muscles were too weak to keep it straight. He agreed and—the surgery was successful. I will never forget that dream fulfilled°I will never forget him for that **IN THE DAYS WHEN I REMEMBER.**

**I did my best to remember those things that my father did that made me feel good**.

I remember him attending my graduation from Kennedy-King City College, in 1987 and my graduation from Wayne State University in 1991. I remember daddy's most recent visit to attend the home going of my 6 month old granddaughter on May 15th of this year. He made every visit special because dad did not often visit me in Detroit...**IN THESE DAYS WHEN I REMEMBER.**

**I did my best to remember those things that my father did that made me feel good**.

I remember standing up to my father, for the first time in my life. I let him know, I knew the difference between wrong and right. I told him "that he was wrong" and I did not take down. I believe he respected me for it; because my dad honored my presence time and time again. This makes me feel good.

As I reminisce, I must share what I have learned over the years. I discovered marriage is an experience where two people come together in mutual respect, appreciation and love. To honor the commitment they vowed to keep, nothing is too good to share with your mate: that bed, that food, that home, **that** a-u-t-o-m-o-b-i-l-e **is your blessing to share with your beloved.**

I learned that a wife is not an object of profanity, ridicule or nay saying. Your children are a heritage of the Lord and neither should you use them as an object of profane words or gestures, of mockery, or malice. I have discovered I am a creature of worth, beauty, strength, love and adoration. I am not designed to be spoken to in a derogatory way, implicit or explicit. I will spend the rest of my life sharing that message, **for this makes me feel REAL GOOD**. As I remember my dad, **I realize how blessed I am**.

IN THE MIRROR Written, August 4, 1998

—I placed this in my two-year old grandson's
obituary.—

W hen I look into the mirror
Who do you think I see?
It is my little grandson, of course
Looking back at me.

I wonder how this happened,
A figment of my imagination?
Our moles and birthmark are in the same
place
This is not, an hallucination.

Just a carbon copy of me,
No matter how I try to hide it…
He is my own reflection
And I can no longer deny it

My reflection serenaded me, one night
On my living room sofa,
This kid was simply incredible,
And now, his suffering is over.

When you see your sister in heaven
Tell her, "I miss her so,"
And tell her brother misses her too
We loved you both, you know.

This morning, I looked in the mirror
Who do you think I saw?
My grandson's strength
His audacity to live
Resting in the hands of God!

<u>YOU SAW THE NEED</u> <u>Written August 11, 1998</u>

—Dedicated to a fine minister; from your sister
in Christ——

𝒴ou saw the need that god—
entrusted to your care,
the reason why, I saw your cards
Attached, in the room somewhere.

You could have said, "Who would know
If I did not do my best,
To visit And pray for this wee lamb?"
But you, did not settle for less.

You made up your mind to rise to the
challenge
Doing your best to obey,
Although my family, were not totally aware
Of the supplications you prayerfully made.

You tipped quietly in the hospital room
Where my little grandson laid,
Doing what god had assigned your hands
Then quietly tipped away.

We did not know, the bond
That you and he formed there,
We were not aware of your sacrifice
Nor how much you really cared.

All I can say is "thank you!"
Only God truly knows my heart
How much I appreciate what you did
I'm so grateful you did your part.

Now I know,
Though he has gone to glory
He was loved and cared for too,
I pray God's anointing keep your family strong
Simply, because, you are you!

THERE IS A SOUND Written August 10, 1998

Prayerfully written by me,
Humbly submitted to our District Elder and his
Elect Lady

I **hear a sound of excitement**
That is moving in the air.
　It is shaking up the elements,
　A sound of genuine care.
　It is a movement in the heavens
　As a might burning fire,
　　The sound of moving forward
　　Of the saints, moving, up higher.
　　It is a sound of progress
　　Of new things happening,
　　　An assurance that God is leading
　　　In this latter-day harvesting.
　　　　Reaching people unreachable,
　　　　Going places we never been,
　　　　　This move of God is troubling
　　　　　People without and within.

There are some of us who do not understand
And feel this is not of God,
　But that is their opinion,

Let His Spirit direct your heart.
Fear, the culprit, has no right
To dictate your longevity,
For God is well able to strengthen you
And your vision, a reality.
Like Moses viewed the Promise Land,
And David, the temple not build,
However, Joshua walked into the Promise
And Solomon, a dream fulfilled.
Bishop David viewed the Promise
And the city he did plan,
But you will walk in the vision
And erect in the Promise Land.
Now if God stays before your face
You will do much more than that,
God will do incredible things for you
His words are not void or slack.
I speak peace into your family
Success in all you do and say,
For your kindness, towards me and mine
Will be remembered for many a day.
Go forward now, young warrior,

Do what God has told you to do
**He will anoint your ministry,
And many will be blessed through
you!**

<u>MY THANKS</u> (For Your Labor of Love)
<u>Written August 12, 1998</u>

My Grandson (1995 – 1998)

—This poem is dedicated to the Children's Hospital Burn Unit, Social Workers, Chaplains and Surgical Waiting Room Staff of Greater Detroit Michigan—

𝒬uietly in your own world
Across the city you come,
To labor with the children,
Burn victims, every one.
From far and near, the children came
Of every race and kind,
Bruised with flames, of some form
So innocent, most of the time.

But on or around the 9th of May
A little fellow entered your wing,
His body burned, 85%
It must have been a horrible thing.
We the family members
Knew not his actual plight,
We only knew we wanted him to live,
We did not choose death, but LIFE.

We did not know about his face,
His arms, legs, abdomen and back;

We all knew he was fighting to live
However, the burns gave him no slack.
When I finally saw him,
I could not hold back the tears,
What had happened to my little man?
Only my worse of fears.

But you saw him on the 9th of May.
You knew what we would later know,
That he would no longer be the same
However, you did not, emotions show.
Each of you proceeded to labor
On my grandson, I could see,
To do the things that were needed
Through the many surgeries.

You were drawn into this scenario,
Predestined to such tragedies;
You were more than a burn unit staff,
You became his family.
Family is there, to help, you see,
They try to ease the pain;
I saw each of you doing your best
To make his life, less of a strain.

Some of you were so good, I marveled
My, what a knowledgeable crew;
Your expertise in this area shown brightly,

I could not stop saying "Thank You"
Thank you so much for listening to me,
When I would grieve within,
Thank you for your every hug;
Thank you for being such a friend.

Thank you for your tolerance—
When I looked on with scrutiny;
I was only a concerned grandmother,
You showed great patience with me.
Thank you for the juice you offered,
Thank you for the snacks;
And for never looking over your shoulder,
When I was having my snack attacks.

For 82 days you struggled
To help him in his plight,
Nurses, doctors, chaplains and other staff
All I wanted was to win this fight.
With all the progress you were making
Skin grafts were healing too,
Some of the problems did not go away
Some of you already knew…

That this child would not make it
The burns would take its toll;
But you, kept on helping him,
Your hearts must be made of gold.

Part Two—Trusting Myself

After the series of code blues,
That really blew my mind;
I for one, could not take much more,
You continued to respond in kind.

> You must have, at times grown weary
> Along such a tedious way;
> Nevertheless, you were there for my baby,
> I do not know quite what to say.
> You were also there for our family
> Especially, my other grandson;
> Bearing with us and bearing with him,
> While he only wanted to have some fun.

When my daughter finally decided
To remove the life support;
You really helped us mightily,
In the remaining time, so short.
I got my first chance to hold him
On, the night before;
You said he really liked this,
I held him 'til my arms were sore.

> However, that did not mean a thing
> I was back for more the next day;
> To see my twin, my little twin,
> Just before he passed away.
> To hold him again, for the very last time
> I did not really know;

I held him until he had gotten worse,
Into your hands he had to go.

Then my baby girl, took her baby
And quietly held him close,
As heartbreaking tears fell from her eyes;
I had to leave, I could take no more.
When I returned, you all were standing there;
Professionals, until the end,
With my little one on oxygen
And little strength to take it in.

    And there, my baby lay so still
    No more movement, no pain or tears;
    My baby was in the arms of God,
    I will miss you, down through the years.
    The staff in The Children's Burn Unit,
    You will miss him too;
    Although I do not know any of your names,
    I think the world of you!

He is with his sister, now.
She is not alone anymore;
He will tell her all you did for him,
The burn unit on the 5th floor.
He will tell her that you loved him,
He will tell her of your care;

He will tell her of your dedication,
In that little room over there.

> I want to hug each of you
> And tell you just how much;
> I pray God's blessing on each of you,
> Cannot seem to say enough.

But, may your homes be filled with laughter
And your children be your source of pride;
May my God above reward each of you,
For taking care, of my little guy.

GREATNESS DEFERRED, Written 8/27/99

—Dedicated to my friend & sister in ministry—

𝒯HERE IT IS!
OH, NO!
ITS—HIDING AGAIN!

Just a glimpse,
  A spark,
    A flicker of light—
  Disappearing
    Into the night.

Oh! There it goes again!
  An intricate part of me
    I've found
      Incredibly hard to see… Most of my life.

It is the GREATNESS within me,
  That has been deferred,
    Because I do not know,
      Who –I- Am.

A part of me,
  To be cognizant of—
    To embrace—
      Through

MUCH DOUBT
And MUCH FEAR.

It is a part
Of me
That is
UNIQUELY ME!
AND
I KNOW
THAT-IT–IS –THERE;

Drawing me,
Calling to me,
Away from whom
I was—
To whom—I am.

It is
Who, I am evolving
Into…
That part
Of
MY EXISTENCE
that…I have denied
MYSELF
Soooo long.

Buried
Soooo deep
And

Longed for
Sooo much;
Since
I
Was
A child.

Too afraid
That
I
Would be
Hated
For
It;
Talked
About
For
It
And
Looked
Down
Somebody's nose —Because —Of —It.

So, I chose instead
To please others
And never me;
And they
Talked
About me still—

Wagging their heads
Behind my back,
  And
  They had no idea
That I sacrificed
THE GREATNESS
  WITHIN ME—
    FOR
        THE GREATNESS
          I SAW
            IN THEM.

Unable to
  Recognize
    That same
      Greatness
        In myself…

So, I strengthened
The **GREATNESS IN OTHERS**,

      Unbeknown
        To me.
          I surrendered a
            Respect
              For who
                I was.

My respect
And love

For others,
Led them
To believe…

I- was
Losing -my -mind,
When I finally
Began to speak
MY OWN CONVICTIONS.

I merely

Relinquished my thoughts
To
EMPOWER
THEIR THOUGHTS Over me.

And occasionally,
when I did find
the strength
to go to a
higher level of thinking
About who
I was.
Someone
would snatch me down
FROM
MY
OVERDUE

PRIVATE
  Celebration of Me;
    Turned
      LOVE AFFAIR
And asked me,
  "JUST WHO
    DO YOU
      THINK
        YOU ARE?"

THERE
IT IS AGAIN!
My newfound friend—
Though now,
Only a fleeting
Moment in my life.

But it will
Slow down—
  It must—
    It is
      My destiny
        And
          My strength.
It is who,
  I always was—
    Although,
      I did not
        KNOW it.

It is what I am—
Destined to become!
As I binge on sweets
As I argue
With myself.
As I try
To explain
MYSELF
To others.
As I
Wag my
Own head
Over my failures
In life,
And over
My
Past-due bills…

I RECOGNIZE THE GREATNESS
WITHIN ME,
Not only shines
But brings
A BEAUTY,
That dazzles, My senses.

I see it
Slowing down.
It must,
It has to Slow down.

I can
   See it,
      But barely see it;
Even
   TOUCH IT,
      But barely —Touch it.

I MUST
Find a way
To EMBRACE IT.

SO –
   I –
      CAN-
                  PLACE–
                     IT–
                        EVER–
SO–
   GENTLY;
            AND QUIETLY
               -IN –MY –OWN –HEART
AND IN
   –MY –OWN –SOUL.

FREELY CARESS IT—
    LOVINGLY EMBRACE IT————

IN ORDER ————-
    TO ————
        TRULY ————
            CELEBRATE —————-
            ME!

IT WAS HIS LOSS!
Written August 28th, 19≈99

—Dedicated to Mr. T. with all my heart!—

"*It* **was his loss!**" I have heard that phrase before.

BUT it was **ONLY RECENTLY**; I heard **its distinctive chime** fall upon **MY** ears.
A genuine, unwavering, though gentle responsiveness to my own
On going inquiry of myself.

"It was HIS loss!" And I wondered only briefly to myself
        —Is it really?
                Then away it flew into the night.

As I drove to my place of work, it is repeated in my ears—
Undeniably, more vibrant than ever before.
"IT WAS HIS LOSS!"
Then with the innocence of a child,
I ask myself
"Is it really **HIS** loss? **How is it HIS LOSS**?
Why is **HIS** rejection of **ME**, **HIS LOSS**?

The words I could barely say to myself,
Much less to anyone else

Stirred my consciousness
Traveled through my heartstrings
Like a youthful waterfall.
I did my best to capture my thoughts—
And not leave them to the mercy of any others.

**It was my love, my tenderness, my warmth,
my sincerity, my intellect**
My hope and dreams
That I offered him.
It was my creativity, insight, understanding,
educational prowess
That I longed to send his way, **alone.**
It was my uniqueness, generosity, and my
prayers I sent up for him.
> **The attention**
> **That he wanted, my awareness**
> **Of him that he needed**
> **That I wish he could have adored and
> ascertained enough**
> **To appreciate me.**
It was the woman I was becoming
I wanted him to see.
Not just the body, he touched…
That alone, was not enough.

**I wanted to fill his throne and throne room
with images of my greatness**

Mingled with his own.
That is what I longed for.

But, there was no such place for me.
There never was! He even told me so.

I knew the truth—
That I never was that high on his
"THINGS-I-NEED-TO-DO LIST."

But I am thankful,
That I still have the will and the strength
To gather up myself
And move on.

I still have a good heart and I have a sound
mind.
I have the strength to pick up the scattered
pieces
Of my creativity, my talents and abilities
My enthusiasm, my spirit
My time, and
My heart.

I am taking it all back
To where it really belonged
In the first place;
With me.

My Personal Reflections

So, I tell myself, don't look back, girl.
He was not the one—no matter **WHAT YOU SAID**
Or **DIDN'T SAY.**
Regardless to **WHAT YOU DID**
Or **DID NOT DO.**
DON'T - LOOK - BACK!

And
No, more regrets!

What wounds that remain
   Are there to remind me;
      I have become A STRONGER WOMAN.

Now, I UNDERSTAND.
   I FINALLY UNDERSTAND!

      IT WAS—*I WAS*—*I AM*—INDEED HIS LOSS!

<u>RECOGNITION</u>   Written 8/20/08

𝒞an you see me?
Really see who I am
Who I am destined to become…
Can you see my inner beauty?
Can you see my heart?
Can you see my desires?
Can you see my sincerity?
Can you see my longings to do
All the great things that are before me….
Can you see me?
Really see me, who I am,
Who I am destined to become....
Can you see?
I am trying to be me.
Can you stand me trying to be me?

No you can't
No you can't possibly
See me, or
See my destiny
See my inner beauty
See my desires and sincerity
See my longings to do and be better
Comprehend the great things that are before me.

See who I really am & destined to become
　　See my efforts to be, me
　　　　No you can't,
　　　　　　Because to know me is to talk to me
And I talk to you.
　　You cannot know me—
　　　　Unless you spend time with me.
　　　　　　To hear my response
　　　　　　　　To really HEAR my response—
　　　　　　　　　　**And comprehend my response,
　　　　　　　　　　to you.**
But that takes time, days, months and years
　　**Of talking, listening, reasoning and
understanding.**
　　　　Too many of us
　　　　　　Do not, cannot—take such time
　　　　　　　　We are too busy, doing important
　　　　　　　　things
　　　　　　　　　　**That are far more interesting
　　　　　　　　　　than....**

"**Lady Please**—**be straight with me**—**For me
to recognize you...**
To see you; to **get to know you; does not
require ALL THAT? Does it???**"

LOVING ME!!!!!   Written 8/20/08

I **think** I have it right
I have finally gotten a grip
I discovered gold
I am the talk of the town

I have it right here
You don't see it? Look closer.
Look closer
You don't see it yet?

You see this little gap in my teeth
It has been called the sexiest thing on me
You see these tiny curly ears
They are so good; I can hear a pin drop on most days

You see these lips
I do not have to put lipstick on
To make other women envy me
But when I do, and it's on just right
I look GOOD!

You see my eyes
Brown on the inside
And grey around the outside
A gorgeous mystery, inherited from my dad

You see my color
Brown with yellow undertones
Like a golden statue
Created by God

You see these ankles
They are so tiny, but they are so strong
And my toes, they have been called cute
By a young podiatrist many years ago

You see this forehead
This is my grandfather; don't tell me he didn't
know what he was doing
You see these strong hands
I can do anything I want to, when I put my mind
to it

**I am loving me—Loving Me—LOVING ME…
until you can see it too!**

YOU, LOVING ME?   Written 8/20/2008

*L*et me tell you—**How to, love me.**

You will see me from a distance
You must look at me until you catch my eye
Keep looking until
You have gotten my attention
  Walk slowly towards me
  Looking at only me
  As you stroll confidently
  You will finally stop in front of me
    Then turn quietly and
    Getting no one's attention but mine
    Stand beside me—enjoying my space
    And let me inhale your quiet manly presence
Say hello very quietly
Saying hello is not hard for me to do
Speak your name in the very same tone
Wait until I turn my attention in your direction
  And look directly into your eyes
  For I will wait until I have your attention
  And my name will roll easily from my lips
  Move closer to my ear and whisper…
    How long you have been noticing me
    And tell me what you saw
    When you looked at me

That had gotten your attention
> **I will listen and enjoy**
> Your every word
> **And steal a glance at you out the corner of my eyes**
> And smile my approval

When I look at you
Look directly in my eyes
Then gently ask me if
You can take my hand
> **I will say, "You may"**
> When you touch my hand
> **Take it ever so gently**
> For I am a delicate flower, and I might just break.

> > **Then face me slowly**
> > Look quietly into my eyes
> > **And ask me gently to give you a chance**
> > To know me better.....

I am a gentle woman, to be handled with great care.
> You only need to look at me to get my attention
> > **You need only to whisper in my ear to ask a question**
> > > I desire only your quiet presence

Only a touch is needed from you to arouse me.

For I am as delicate as china——today and tomorrow—

And to the soothing man,

Who is sincere,

Who has a quiet confidence

Whose courtesy truly defines him

Who dares to believe that he is my covering

Who is willing to share himself

Who is willing to open his heart

Who is truly

Ready to love <u>only</u> me…

Who only wants

What I can offer

What I can give him

And cherish all that

And adore me too…

For the rest of my life and his

Because he is truly

Ready to love me only...

He need ONLY...TO...APPLY.

<u>YOU—MISS ME?</u> <u>Written December 19, 2008</u>

This is my reflections three months after I went to Maryland to meet my new daughter-in-law. My ex-husband was there, like me, to witness his son saying his marriage vows. Up until this time, my son's father had this habit of when seeing me of saying "you know, I still miss you"—or something to that affect. I did not quite get it, his pitiful look, his somberness, when saying those words. I often felt, why is he saying that; to make me feel sorry, to make me feel good? Get me to smile—(All of us want to feel good.) But, I think I have it NOW. This is my response.

*Y*OU, MISS ME? Exactly why do you miss me?

Do you miss slapping me across
The face-because-you-felt-I-was-insolent or something…?
Or do you miss grabbing my hands when I was trying unsuccessfully to fight you back?
Do you miss putting knives to my throat, guns to my back and threatening my life?

YOU SAID YOU MISS ME? Exactly how do you miss me?

Maybe you miss turning my eyes black and blue with your fist
On this light-brown skin.
Or as you called it "YOUR HALF WHITE ASS"
Maybe you miss my tears when you were relentless in your accusations
Though I tried to wife them away... I mean wipe them away...
Ever so quietly, so you did not get upset again....

YOU, MISS ME? Exactly when did you miss me?
Was it the first, second, or the third time I left you and that house?
Nope. It was definitely the **fourth time**!
BECAUSE I DID NOT RETURN...DID NOT LOOK BACK...DID NOT HAVE ANY REGRETS....
But I ALMOST believed you, when you told me..."-NO-ONE-WOULD-WANT-MY-STUPID ASS!"

Yeap! It was definitely the fourth time!
You missed your punching bag!
You missed you floor mat!

My Personal Reflections

You missed our precious time together…
When you threw my freshly cooked food on the floor…
Threw my naked body out the bed…
Pinned my body down on the floor, OR
In the bed, OR
On the wall while you hurled your debilitating names and threats at me
Close range.…
Because you knew, I could not, get away.

Maybe you miss rubbing you hand across the table or door posts
To see if there was any dust LEFT
Anywhere in that house.

OH, I KNOW…
Perhaps you missed showing my children
What **A REAL MAN WAS LIKE** and
WHAT A STUPID, GOOD-FOR NOTHING GETTING-WHAT-YOU-DESERVE-WOMAN WAS LIKE…
Teaching and re-teaching **THOSE TERRIBLE lessons**
To our precious son and daughter
What the future held for them—
With my reluctant
(IT IS WHAT IT IS-NO-LESS)

P-A-R-T-I-C-I-P-A-T-I-O-N.

YOU **MISS ME?**   Exactly what are you missing?

My submission to you.

  My fear of you

    My quietness with you

      My toleration of you

        My obedience to you

          My distress

        My agony

          My torture from you

No! You miss

  ⇒ **YOUR SUPREMACY**

  ⇒ **YOUR   MISSTAKEN   IDEA   OF MANHOOD**

  ⇒ **YOUR   MISCONSCREWED   INTER PRETATION OF GREATNESS**

  ⇒ **YOUR SELF-PROCLAIMED KINGSHIP**

        WHICH WERE BASED ON

          • **My Inferiority**

          • **My Fragility**

          • **My Weakness** and

          • **My Servitude**!

YOU

    DO

      NOT

      REALLY

        MISS

          ME!

YOU- JUST- MISS- HAVING-SOMEONE -TO-PICK- ON

BECAUSE- THE -BITCH –YOU- NOW- HAVE WON'T -LET -YOU....

YOU DO NOT MISS ME—
YOU MISS THOSE LIFE-CHANGING MOMENTS YOU HAD—
THAT MADE YOU FEEL
THE WAY
YOU THINK A MAN MUST FEEL.

YOU REALLY DO NOT MISS ME!
YOU MISS THAT VERSION OF ME, THAT
YOU THOUGHT YOU HAD,
IN THE PALM OF YOUR HAND

YOU MISS THAT CRAZY FOOL
WHO STAYED WITH YOU
ALL THOSE YEARS
JUST BECAUSE
SHE REFUSED
TO BELIEVE IN HERSELF....

WELL,
   THAT
         WOMAN…
            YOU
               KNEW—
OR
   THOUGHT…
                  YOU
                     KNEW—
DOES
   NOT
         LIVE

               HERE
                  ANY
                     MORE…
               AND…
         THE-
LAST-TIME I SAW HER…SHE ELUDED
TO THE FACT THAT

S-H-E-   HAS   <u>N-O</u>—F-O-R-W-A-R-D-I-N-G A-D-D-R-E-S-S…!!!!!!!

<u>NOTHING LIKE IT!</u> <u>Written February 20, 2009</u>

*T...*here is
Nothing like a Man
To make a woman
Like me,
Feel Good!

    *N*othing **like a Man**
    To tell me,
    "I like your outfit"
    When I feel
    I could look better.

        *N*othing **like a Man**
        Who tells me
        "I love
        The way you smell"
        When I
        Least expect it!

        *N*othing **like a Man**
        Who tells me
        "Your hair
        Is beautiful Sister"
        To make me
        Glow all over!

There is nothing
Like a Man
Giving me
A GREAT BIG HUG
At a moment
When I
Need it most!

Nothing quite
Like a Man
Asking me
"May I
Kiss your hand?"
Because he says
My presence leaves
Him speechless!

There is Nothing
Like a Man
Opening a car door
For me,
Without me
Asking him to!

There really is
Nothing like a Man
Opening a car door
For me

When no one else
Is looking!
    *T*here **is nothing**
    Like a Man
    Whispering
    In my ear
    His appreciation
    For Me!
        *T*here **is nothing**
        Like a man
        Holding my hand,
        Just because…

*T*here **is nothing**
Like a Man
Who is
Not afraid
To say
"I love you!"

        *T*here **is nothing**
        Like a Man
        Who has
        Found
        His True
        Soul Mate
        And
        Treasures Her!

There is Absolutely,
Unequivocally,
Nothing Like It!

So, while I wait
For him; to come…
Who will proclaim
His Love and Respect
For me...
There is nothing,
Like—Loving
And Respecting Myself!
There is Non-confoundedly;
Unapologetically,
Nothing, Like It!

Lady Day is the mother of two adult children, a son and a daughter. She has 7 grandchildren between them. A terrible apartment fire claimed the lives of two others in 1998. Her mother is 88 years old and still resides in the Chicago land area, along with Lady Day's three remaining siblings. She holds three degrees and has worked 18 years for the Detroit Public School (DPS) system. A high school teacher for 15 years, Lady Day retired officially from DPS on July 1, 2009 due to on-going health issues. Raised and nurtured in the Apostolic faith, she only wishes to be a comfort to God's people. She is learning "to her own self be true"; and for the first time, to trust herself. She endeavors in this, her first book, to "…WRITE THE VISION AND MAKE IT PLAIN UPON TABLES, THAT HE MAY RUN THAT READETH IT." Habakkuk 2:2.

Made in the USA
Lexington, KY
26 July 2017